"As people read the book they will be resurrecting energy that is necessary within themselves to transform."
—Cecilia Ampon

"Gil offers a way for people to step out of the box of old beliefs, in a gentle and honest way by taking them through his journey. His stories and allegories are painted with the patience of a wise spiritual teacher so a greater picture of understanding can be grasped by the student. And those who are ready, will."
—Suzanne Taylor

"These amazing revelations make the teachings relatable and possible for everyone."
—Helen Delaney

"My heart chakra was so open through the whole experience and full of love and joy! It was like coming home to who I truly am. All the past guilt, sadness, and self-destructive thoughts were freed. Gil's thoughts and words help release the destructive chains of the ego to the beauty of truth."
—Polly Campbell

"We are living in a time when anyone can write about their spiritual experiences without judgment and persecution. In the past, as even Gil noted in this excerpt, one could be beheaded for making the claim that we are God. In my past study I've read many accounts of many such claimants who have been persecuted in Christianity and Islam and from this cursory reading of what Gil has to say I feel what he is conveying is very much in alignment with what some of these greatest of Saints have also taught. I appreciate the parables and metaphors he uses and I appreciate how he leaves the responsibility and choice to the individual as to how and when they pursue their path while assuring them that if they are ready that every spiritual assistance they could ever need is at their disposal."

—Shahiroz

"This book is not for the faint-hearted reader… It is an energy insertion that expands the span of limitation that people live within and gives you a higher level of understanding from the balcony of Spirit."

—Amalia Camateros

"There is no feeling here from Gilbert of pride in his yogic achievements but more the power of sitting quietly before God in a state of surrender and wonder. As a reader, that message is very inspirational and will help [people] to feel that this is a path with an enlightened outcome that is available to them. This is a very strong and impactful message that, put in Gil's simple and accessible wording and brought to life by his stories, makes the spiritual path look accessible and intriguing to potential seekers."

—Kathleen McLaughlin

AWAKEN TO THAT WHICH WE ARE

*You Shall Know the Truth
and the Truth Will Set You Free*

AWAKEN TO THAT WHICH WE ARE

*You Shall Know the Truth
and the Truth Will Set You Free*

GIL ESQUIBEL
with Ashleigh F. Torres

The Awakened Press

The Awakened Press

For information about special discounts or for bulk purchases, please contact The Awakened Press at books@theawakenedpress.com.

The Awakened Press can bring authors to your live event. For more information or to book an event contact books@theawakenedpress.com or visit our website at www.theawakenedpress.com.

Book editors, Ashleigh F. Torres and Lindsay R.A. Dierking
Cover and book design by Kurt A. Dierking II

Printed in the United States of America
First The Awakened Press trade paperback edition

ISBN: 979-8-9881800-5-0

CONTENTS

Foreword by Ashleigh F. Torres   v

Introduction   ix

Chapter 1   The Journey into Enlightenment   1

Chapter 2   Who Is God?   11

Chapter 3   The Early Journey   21

Chapter 4   The Ego   29

Chapter 5   Unraveling the Ego   45

Chapter 6   The Search for Truth   55

Chapter 7   The Obstacle of Pride   67

Chapter 8   Free Will or Destiny?   75

Chapter 9   Prayer   89

Chapter 10   The Death of Illusion   101

Chapter 11   Forgiving the Illusion   115

Chapter 12   The Inner Child and Innocence   135

Chapter 13   Letting Go   145

The Summit   157

Recommended Resources and Further Reading   161

Gil Esquibel   163

This book is dedicated to my brother and friend Jeshua Ben Joseph, who has guided me from the beginning to the end of my spiritual journey.

I honor the Sacred Feminine; Mother Mary; Mary Magdalene; Cecilia Ampon; my sister in the Light, Crystal; and my spiritual oracles who played key roles along my journey.

I am grateful to all my teachers, known and unknown.
Even though I may not have seen you as teachers at the time,
I understand that life is a classroom and I am very grateful
and honored for all the lessons that you brought into my life.

I want to thank my first spiritual teacher, Father Paul Blighton, who was very instrumental in opening the doors of enlightenment for me.
He was a very bright light who opened spiritual doors for many.

I am very grateful to Sri AmmaBhagavan, living Avatars in India, God Realized, who have been instrumental during this final stage of my journey.

I am grateful to Clayten Stedman, whose high level of knowledge and skill in calibrating levels of consciousness provided me with a deeper understanding throughout the years of my process.
Thank you for your contribution in my life and to this book.

I dedicate this book to all the children that have been born and all those children who will be born. May this wisdom help you in this world and give you resources to carry the light forward into future generations.
I love you Alyra and Astaria.

Thank you to our editor Lindsay and publisher at The Awakened Press for your commitment, attention to detail and care to make this book available to all those seeking greater spiritual enlightenment.

I acknowledge and thank my late wife Linda, who was a loving foundation for me and continues to illuminate and grace my life as one of my guides.

I dedicate this book to my wife Ashleigh.
Your integrity to this book, your editing and the channels you opened for the release of this book have been invaluable.
Thank you for your devotion, friendship and most of all, your selfless love.
You have supported me to thrive in this 3D world in ways I normally would not have and I thank you from the depth of my heart.

The use of the word God is frequent in this book.
It is important for you to understand that people differentiate from their beliefs, culture and upbringing as to their personal understanding of what God is to them.

What does God mean in the context of this book?

God is an Infinite, All-Knowing, Loving Consciousness.
God works through individuals in a way that
resonates with their understanding.

Many people at this point do not recognize the Oneness of all life.

This book is intended to enlighten the mind
as to what God is to each individual.

No "one way" is the better way.
This is simply the author's way.

God is a beautiful, Expansive Energy of Oneness,
which is All Within Us.
At some point, this Oneness will weave us all together.

The use of the word asleep and/or sleep is used throughout this book.
This is used symbolically.

The word recognizes that we have separated
from the consciousness of God.

When we separate from the consciousness of God,
we liken that to being asleep.

When we start to unite with the consciousness of God,
we liken this to the beginning of Awakening.

Foreword

The first time I met Gil was in Sedona, Arizona in 2012. He walked into an art gallery I worked in, and time suspended for three hours. During this period in my life, I was in formal disciplined meditation twenty-five hours a week where part of our practice was to measure our time in that process. As a result of this, I was sensitive to high energy fields. I was curious as I observed and felt a very clear person with a high vibratory atmosphere around him. His energy had a pristine quality in a way I had never experienced before. I observed a completely uncluttered soul that was very aware of itself as consciousness.

As Gil and I spent time together, it was an otherworldly experience that involved many incarnations together and soul recognitions in our shared devotion for God. For the first few years, we shared a long-distance relationship in which we visited each other on a regular basis and shared daily phone conversations. We discovered the same values in life, a shared love and adoration for God, along with similar spiritual goals. Years later, we shared one home and a wonderful community of friends and family.

There was the deepest familiarity and trust for one another that was neither warranted nor understood in present time. This soul recognition would supersede many challenges we would work through during our spiritual union.

Over the course of eleven years, each of us experienced an unfoldment of ancient divine love.

Sometimes on an Earth level it was a struggle, this perceived process of

Enlightenment or Christ Consciousness Gil was experiencing, as the process didn't fit into a recognizable mental framework for me. Spiritual concepts of enlightenment can sometimes cause us this internal struggle or internal confusion but in the end, all there is, is Love...and I was reminded this was something so Divine that we could share.

Sometimes I was prompted by doubts and the internal struggles of the human condition and I did find myself challenging him at many turns as he consistently remained open minded, single focused, aligning his will with complete surrender into God's will. I witnessed Gil, clear, unencumbered and pure of heart with a silent flow of power that I experienced like a magic carpet when I was in his energy fields, where everything continually flowed.

Witnessing Gil's transformation into God Consciousness has been a critical factor in my spiritual development as a soul. Gil effortlessly poured meaning and understanding while I contemplated deep spiritual principles and all my attachments with such clarity, resulting in progressive shifts in my consciousness. We are all human, after all, but we search for the Divine within ourselves.

The steady unfoldment of our union gifted us with an annihilation of our egos and an extraordinary process together which continues to inform.

Living in his energy fields of deep stillness and peace would cause me to have spiritual experiences. During one experience, I involuntarily dropped to my knees in pure bliss, feeling Gil's potent union with God. My soul recognized a certain resonance in Gil's energy fields through my own devotional experiences with God. Auspicious accounts, coupled with his divine connection, led my heart to embody a powerful conviction that this was definitely a holy man, yet to the outer world he was a simple, kind, unassuming person.

Gil's state of consciousness, linked with God's Emmanent Grace working through me and with me, was so potent that a natural progression of transformation occurred in me from experiencing Gil's daily process, rendering me free from the grip my fears held fast to and what I had believed truth to be. In our union, I have come into a new understanding of authentic love and freedom of the heart.

My experience in witnessing the Enlightenment and/or Christ Consciousness process has also taught me that we are still in a human body with human limitations. What a humbling experience to trust the process of the perceived human limitations while acknowledging you are One with God.

The concept of limitations can sometimes be challenging for one experiencing God Consciousness to accept, and can be misrepresented as ego and spiritual bypassing.

I fell into this misrepresented judgment, until I embodied a different level of understanding through time and through my sincere desire to see beyond my own limitations.

Gil is rare to have never accepted limitations to enter his conscious mind. This may have been a key factor toward his realization.

I witnessed Gil's unshakeable faith and single focus, manifesting his life into higher and higher energy fields, while dismantling all that was false, transcending his belief systems and his identifications. Over time and through these writings you can witness Gil's mental, emotional and spiritual relationship to everything, shaping how he came into his present state, through God's pure Grace.

Delve into Gil's process and journey, embodying Pristine Inner Stillness, Unconditional Love and the ability to balance a formless life in what we perceive as form and limited.

I bow to the God in Gil, I bow to the God in us all.

I bow to you, the reader, as you engage in this and may the Supreme Consciousness Which Sustains the Universe guide you and bless you.

—Ashleigh F. Torres

Introduction

**YOU ARE TOTALLY FREE,
YOU HAVE NEVER DONE ANYTHING WRONG.
YOU ARE ONLY DREAMING.
TO FULLY AWAKEN FROM THIS DREAM,
YOU MUST BE WILLING TO LET GO OF THIS ILLUSION
AND ALL IDENTIFICATION WITH YOUR ILLUSIONARY SELF.**

Throughout this book I will be sharing this same truth over and over in many different ways, seeking to have this truth become a sacred knowing in the mind of the reader. I will give you many different examples of this truth so that by the time you finish this book, your understanding of truth will be expanded to the point of freeing you from the false egoic belief system. So this book, for many, will be like seeds planted in the consciousness of your mind. As you begin to awaken spiritually, you will come to the realization that you have always been loved by God more than you can ever begin to imagine, no matter what you believe you have done. The timing for our soul development is always in divine order and everything we experience is sacred and holds value.

We are in a very important and critical time here on Earth in which this planet is going through frequency and consciousness expansion from the third dimension into the fifth dimension and higher. The difference between dimensions are different levels of consciousness. My purpose for writing this book is to help prepare many for this transformation. There will be many who are not yet ready for this transformative event. Eventually, all souls will return to the Oneness. There is no limit to the time frame in which this will happen.

There will be things shared in this book that will deeply challenge the belief system of the egoic mind. I will admit that as a person ascends on the spiritual path, he will run into a number of conundrums (riddles without an answer to the conscious mind). I will try to shed light on these conundrums so that the reader will be able to have an understanding of what is required to make the leap from illusion to reality.

As some of you already know, when a person reaches a state of full spiritual awakening, he or she will understand that the world we believed was real is simply a very vivid dream we are having and in reality never did exist. Everything that ever seemed to happen, everything that seems to be happening now, or will happen in the future in the physical universe, is in fact an illusion. The question is: how far down the rabbit hole are we willing to go?

There is another part to this conundrum of living in this dream world, which is that there is a powerful cosmic purpose for going through this illusion. Those who have voluntarily chosen to enter the darkness and illusion of this world are very brave and bold adventurers. The contribution they are making to the expansion of creation and to the nature of God is unprecedented and priceless.

My personal journey has been a relationship with the Christ Consciousness. I want to share with you that **Christ Consciousness *means Union with God*** and this union can be accomplished through different spiritual paths.

Throughout this book I will use the name Jeshua instead of Jesus because this was his name when he walked the earth: Jeshua Ben Joseph, which is Aramaic.

Another reason for using the name Jeshua instead of Jesus is that the name Jesus has been so misrepresented in religious doctrine that much of the pure truth he brought into Earth has been lost in the dogma of religion. Let me also add that Jeshua does not in any way desire to be worshiped or looked on as someone superior. He wants to be seen as our brother and friend. Jeshua knows that we are all one and unified in God.

We have so many concepts, opinions, desires, belief systems and identifications that keep the truth buried deep within our minds. Discovering and dissolving these false beliefs and identifications is the purpose of the spiritual journey so that we can realize who we truly are. When we are ready to awaken, we enter a spiritual path that takes us on a journey of awakening to the realization that we are One with God. This is what Jeshua meant when he said that a person must give up his life to find life (Matthew 16:24-26). When that which is false is eliminated, the truth will shine forth and we will awaken to the glory that we are One with God.

The light and love within us will reveal that everything that seemed to take place in this world is actually an illusory dream that has no reality. There is no need to feel guilty about anything. In reality, you are innocent and have never done anything wrong. This is an absolute truth which will fully be realized by all souls upon their awakening. This truth will be very difficult to comprehend for those deeply caught up in the darkness of illusion. They will have to climb out of that darkness to begin to allow the light of Truth to enter their hearts and minds in order to begin waking up. Even in that deep darkness, they are perfectly innocent and have never done anything wrong. They are simply caught up in a dark dream from which they are having a very hard time awakening. There are many now walking the earth who have awakened and are allowing the Light within them to shine into the one mind. This is opening the way for those stuck in darkness an opportunity to also awaken in this day and age.

When we reach a state of realizing the real purpose of our journey on Earth, the concept of judging others will completely disappear. We are all innocent; we always have been and always will be. The intellectual mind and individuality will not be able to comprehend this truth because the limited mind perceives things through the filter of the egoic mind, which is limitation, judgment and separation. The false ego cannot possibly conceive of infinity, pure love and oneness.

The intent of this book is to help awaken the state of innocence and oneness in all who seek it. Accepting Our Innocence is a very necessary step on the path to our awakening. It is not something we have to earn, it is our birthright. It is our very nature. The false ego, which you will read about in this book, will do everything in its power to keep us from accepting our innocence. Please note that any reference to the ego in this book will be referring to the false, unbalanced ego unless noted otherwise. Our pure Ego is a positive and necessary aspect of who we are. It is when it becomes unbalanced and takes over our lives that it becomes a destructive force. We all have the ability to bring our egos back into balance so that we can become a great light for others.

Our spiritual journey will ultimately lead us to a realization that both the light and dark elements of life are two halves of a whole and we will transcend the idea of duality. The very nature of creation is that whenever we have a positive force there is an equally negative force to counterbalance it.

We gave the ego the power to take over our lives when we first began this journey into illusion. When we are ready, we begin the process of waking up and dissolving the illusionary ego. This ego led us on the path of fear and guilt, which resulted in this dream we are having. Currently, because of the lack of understanding in this world, dissolving the ego, for many, is not even a possibility, much less a desire. This is not a judgment; it simply reflects the current conditions of the consciousness now present on Earth at this time.

Beyond this world of illusion there is an Existence, which is so much greater than our wildest dreams here on Earth. **The greatest goal, and the only true goal, is for a person to wake up spiritually and discover who he or she truly is.** It has nothing to do with your state of affairs in the world. It has to do with discovering the sacred truth of who you are. This discovery will lead us face to face with the knowing that we are One with God. We are greater than we can ever even begin to imagine with our intellect, because our intellect cannot imagine such greatness. Nevertheless, this is who we are. The ultimate destiny of all who have ever walked the earth is to realize and experience our oneness with God. I hope my message, throughout this book, will be a light on the path for all who read it.

What I have written may be new concepts for some, so I have used many analogies and stories so the reader can more easily grasp the essence of what is being written. The Teacher who taught me and prepared me is not of this world. This Teacher, who is in all of us, is just waiting for us to make the decision to know the truth. The Teacher I am referring to is the Holy Spirit. The Holy Spirit has nothing to do with Christianity or religion. In *A Course in Miracles*, for example, the Holy Spirit is described as "Right Mindfulness." The term "Holy Spirit" is also known as the "Inner Self" or "Divine Consciousness." Any true spiritual master is part of the mind of the Holy Spirit. The Holy Spirit is that part of our mind we share with God. The Holy Spirit is buried deeply in the minds of many people but can never be lost completely. When we are ready, the Holy Spirit allows us to remember what we have forgotten, which is our perfection, innocence and oneness with God.

I have used "him" and "her" interchangeably throughout this book. When we reach our final destination, we will find that male and female do not exist in the way we think about it here on Earth. When a person reaches a certain state of spiritual realization, the awareness that each one of us contains both the Divine male and female aspects in perfect balance will be realized. Consequently, I have occasionally interspersed a question-and-answer format in anticipation to questions I felt would be in the minds of many of the readers.

There are many paths that lead to spiritual enlightenment. A person might ask, "Who would I be if I gave up myself?" That's a great and very important question and the answer is very simple: You would be yourself, only without all the darkness and guilt. Most people constantly carry darkness and guilt with them. A powerful spiritual statement is: **"I am that I am."** This is a sacred and holy statement that you might want to ponder upon. The true you can never die as you are as eternal as God.

My spiritual journey was a very long and difficult one. I always believed that I would reach my spiritual destination, but there were many, many times that my path seemed very dark and hopeless. I have lived through a full and wide variety of earthly, human experiences. Covering a span of life ranging from early childhood trauma, serving the military, becoming a spiritual nondenominational priest, serving as a financial analyst for the U.S. Treasury, to sharing a marriage of twenty-nine years, I learned that these did not define who I was.

I went through periods of questioning whether my goal was just a fantasy in my mind. None of us will travel the same path. For some, the road will be much smoother than for others, but there is one thing that all who have reached the "Promised Land" will have in common: **Each one that reaches this state of consciousness will have voluntarily relinquished their own personal ego, which consists of the identification and attachment to the limited and flawed individual we believe we are.** I hope this book will give you a much greater understanding of what the false ego is, because it is always best to understand your biggest adversary which is constantly trying to trick you into believing that it is who you are.

Our scientific discoveries in the field of quantum physics are now doing more than many religions to help mankind find the truth. Quantum physicists have discovered that what appears to be the concrete world is really all happening in our mind. In other words, the world we seem to live in is not real. It is a figment of our imagination. Albert Einstein summed up this idea in his statement, "Reality is merely an illusion, albeit a very persistent one." Science will never be able to fully reveal what the truth is, but quantum physics is helping people release their concepts of what we consider to be the "concrete world" and thus helping people prepare themselves for a deeper understanding of reality. Letting go of false concepts is a necessary part in remembering what is real.

Another revealing finding in quantum physics is that each one of us is responsible for creating our own reality through our beliefs, choices, desires, thoughts, and emotions. Quantum physicists have also discovered that time is not linear and that on the quantum level a person could just as easily go backward or forward in time. An amazing world of possibilities has been revealed through quantum physics. Our spiritual development will bring all of this into greater clarity and understanding. Full spiritual awakening brings about the realization that God and you are One.

We all have the memory of the whole truth within us. Trust that the truth within you will lead you home. Jeshua said, "You shall know the truth and the truth shall set you free" (John 8:31-32). As the truth of who we are begins to dawn in our minds, through the dis-identification with the false self, we realize that we have the power within us to totally transform our minds and lives completely. It is up to us and depends on how much we want it.

What I am writing about is beyond the concept of our individual ego, since the individual ego is an illusion that, in truth, never existed. I will put this truth in as simple a way as possible to allow you to see the way home—here is an analogy that symbolizes what I am talking about throughout these chapters: imagine a huge warehouse that is lit by a single bright light. Now imagine that after many, many years the light started being dimmed by the grime and dirt that floated throughout the warehouse. After many, many more years, the light was completely covered by dirt so that very little light could be seen. A janitor was called in to clean the dirt off the light.

The dirt represents the false ego that we have believed in for so long. A large portion of the population on Earth has been so blinded by the ego that there is very little Light left to see the truth. The message I am relaying is how to start releasing the belief in the ego, which is the darkness that covers your Light. The janitor represents your efforts to wake up from this illusion by cleaning your vision through the renouncing of the egoic mind.

Be patient and sincere with yourself in your efforts to remember who you truly are. The spiritual journey will lead you to the full realization that there is only God and we are That.

—Gil Esquibel

One

The Journey into Enlightenment

I began having some of my most profound spiritual experiences about twenty-five years ago. I had many meditation instances during this time in which I experienced, without a doubt, the absolute truth that I was One with God, pure and holy in every way. It was not only a realization of who I am, but an expression of a divine state of being which eventually brought about the complete dissolution of the illusory self.

The many, many occurrences of this Oneness would happen in a very sacred way. I would sit for meditation and suddenly, within seconds, the consciousness of Gil and the life I was living as a so-called "individual" would fade into the background. I would look at the life of Gil from a state of Oneness with the absolute knowing that this individual person never existed. It was so astonishing to have this absolute knowing that this person, with all his issues, who I had identified with for most of my life, was not real. Imagine what it would be like to experience the truth: that the person you thought you were was never real. This actualization and realization is the doorway into enlightenment.

These realizations soon became a continuous reality in my life. I found it very fascinating to walk in two worlds at the same time. My realization about my Oneness with God became more constant, along with my knowing that the world of illusion never actually happened. I then understood the words of Jeshua when he walked on this Earth: **"I am in the world but not of it"** (John 17:15-16).

When I first started having these experiences, I was still caught up in the life of Gil, thinking he was real. During meditations at this time, Gil and the whole illusion of the world would very quickly dissolve, within seconds, into the nothingness from whence they seemed to have come. I would instead take on the consciousness of my Oneness with God. I have had this realization and embodiment many, many times and I am now moving into a state where I feel it is becoming permanent. In this state, I would talk to God or Jeshua, or other great beings, just as if I were talking to my closest friends and I absolutely knew that they were hearing me.

There was a connection in consciousness and even without seeing them, I knew I was with them. There was always a beautiful radiance and otherworldly feeling of Oneness with God, Jeshua, and other great beings as this was occurring, and there was a bright white light around my head. I now see this light around my head throughout my daily life.

I now constantly experience the great reality that I am God walking this Earth in this body. I also have the realization that everyone and everything in creation is God. There is a sacred Oneness on all levels of creation and in all dimensions, and this Oneness is the Mind of God. Please do not think that I am being prideful or egotistical when I proclaim that I am God, because this reality applies to you and to everyone and everything in creation. We are God but we have fallen into a deep sleep and forgotten who we are. Instead, we are dreaming that we are this individual character which, in reality, has no existence. For the great majority of those on Earth, this idea that I am presenting seems absurd. A person has to be very spiritually open to fully embody this truth and I believe that there are many on Earth who have already begun this embodiment process.

After a few years of having many of these occurrences, the identity of Gil has completely dissolved and there is now a very different, more enlightened consciousness inhabiting this body. These events were so sacred and beautiful, that to describe them in mere words minimizes their sacredness. During one of these meditations, I experienced the descent of the Holy Spirit into me in the form of a ball of white light. As this was happening, I was prompted by the spirit to say out loud, **"The descent of the Holy Spirit."** Initially, I didn't say anything, and I was again prompted to say the phrase out loud, which I then spoke. I feel that the purpose of having me say this out loud was to impress in my mind the importance of this experience.

If you know yourself to be God, then wouldn't all things be possible to you?

It is a soul's purpose—why he or she entered the world—which would determine the gifts they are given. When a soul reaches the state of God Realization, he or she may appear to be a normal person and yet they carry the great Light of that Realization into the mind of the world and help to more fully enlighten it without saying a word. There have been many sages in India, living in caves, who have manifested this truth. Others may have a purpose to be known as spiritual teachers and thus are given certain gifts particular to that purpose. I have been shown what my purpose for coming into the world is and how that will manifest.

I had many actualizations which revealed to me very clearly that our separation from God never really occurred and that the separation was, in fact, impossible. The first time I knew this to be true, I had to start laughing at the absurdity of our belief in this world as being real. During some of these meditations, I actually stepped outside the illusion of time and space and felt the essence of its unreality in a way that was so clear and comprehensible that my perception of the world completely changed.

In my experiences of Oneness with God, there was still a relationship between God and me. This could be referred to as "The Mystical Marriage" or to one who has reached the state of Christhood. There is a union in this state of Oneness between God, or Love, and the uniqueness of your soul, the I AM THAT I AM, which is and will always be the truth of who we are as God in manifested form. **When a person reaches a certain state of spiritual realization he will experience and realize that the God he was seeking is actually himself.** In a recent meditation, I saw myself approaching the tabernacle on the altar in which the symbol of God was kept for spiritual services. I walked up to the tabernacle and slowly opened the door and what I saw was my own self sitting on the throne in the tabernacle. It was a really amazing revelation of who, in reality, we are. We will all see and have the same experience as we journey toward Christ Consciousness. We will then know that we are God. We will have come to a full realization that there is only one thing in all of creation and that is God, so you can only be God, otherwise you would not exist. I have fully actualized this reality within myself and know absolutely that this is the greatest truth of all. When a person fully experiences and accepts this, he will have reached a state of Union with God. There must be a complete relinquishment of the state of mind that experiences itself as a separate entity and the belief in duality and separation in any way. Only God exists and thus to have existence, we must be a part of God. The essence of the spiritual journey is to relinquish that which never had an existence in the first place so that we can awaken to the great Truth of who we are.

Knowing that the person we have identified with is not real will only be philosophy until a person gets down to the task of renouncing and releasing that which has kept them bound to the illusion. Until a soul has reached a state of realization, in which they can embody a full conviction that, **"I am the One I have been seeking,"** it will only be a philosophy. Be patient with yourself and this moment of full realization will come to those who are willing to release the false egoic self that holds them back from the great realization that you are God walking the Earth. **The essence of what it is we have to release is our belief that we are this individual and that we are separate from God and each other.** There are different approaches to help in dissolving our false identity that keeps us separate from God and each other and I will expound on these in later chapters. The main desire a person must have to accomplish this task is the total desire to do whatever is necessary to know the Truth of who she is, which will set her free. Unless a person has this overwhelming desire to know this truth, it will remain only a philosophy and nothing else. There is nothing wrong with a soul taking as long as they desire to begin this journey to God Realization. You have free will and it is your choice. Just let me ask you: would you prefer pain and loneliness, or infinite Joy, Peace, and Love? It is your decision and only yours. The complete relinquishment of the ego is not for the faint of heart as it does entail the death of everything you thought you were.

According to spiritual teachers like David R. Hawkins, M.D., Ph.D., many souls turn back when they come to this final gate of coming into union with all that is. I would assume that they turn back because of the continued attachment to some part of the egoic self and the fear of losing it. It could also be the fear of the Unlimited Reality of who we are. At this point, the soul is not quite ready to look at, or accept the reality of the Infinite Light that we are. It is still too much Light and very scary to fully accept that we are God. As the saying goes, **"Light is the darkness most feared."**

There is a consciousness within us, which is truly who we are, that has been completely forgotten by most souls on Earth at this time. That consciousness is called the **"I Am That I Am"** within you. This is the real you that can never be lost; it is your connection with God, with your true Self. **You are the I AM THAT I AM right now.** You only have to give up a false belief system that has been running the show for so long. **It is time to wake up and not be deluded into thinking you are just an individual person seeking to find safety in an illusionary world. When you wake up, you will find that you are still you, except without all the sense of separateness and weakness that make up the false egoic self.** You will wake up to see and experience that you have all Love, Bliss and Joy available to you at all times for all eternity.

Imagine that the most beautiful painting ever painted entitled "The Light" was misplaced in some dark cave for thousands and thousands of years. There was still some talk about the painting in present time, but most people thought it was only a fairy tale and not real. One man believed this painting was real and continually searched for it for many years. He traveled the world looking for it and one glorious day he was intuitively led to an old cave in one of the far corners of the world. As he searched the cave, he did not recognize the painting immediately as it was covered with layer upon layer of dirt and mildew. Something at the core of his being told him that this was the original painting of The Light. The excitement in him was overwhelming. He knew he would have to be very careful in removing the heavy layers of dirt and grime so as to not damage the painting. Finally, after many years of tedious work, the full restoration of the painting was complete. He so wanted to share this incomparable work with everyone and so he spent the rest of his life traveling to share "The Light" with all who were interested in the greatest work of art ever created.

This story is, of course, analogous to the search for God Realization within each of us. This is a long and arduous journey but the Love and Joy that comes with the realization of who you truly are is incomparable. There is nothing that could even be compared to it.

The spiritual experiences I have been having opened my consciousness to a completely new way of perceiving the world and how I experienced my own self. I am forever grateful to Jeshua, my teacher, for his guidance throughout my spiritual journey. In another experience and vision, I stood outside the realm of time and saw the whole physical universe as a very small mist, which quickly dissipated into nothingness in the presence of a very bright sunshine. The bright sunshine is, of course, representative of the awakened consciousness.

The statement that the illusion of the world is unreal and actually never happened is true and yet this experience of the illusion adds something to the glory of creation and is absolutely sacred. An appropriate analogy is to imagine a tree that grows a fruit that is poison to anybody that partakes of it. Now imagine that scientists find a way of processing this fruit and diluting it in a number of steps which takes the poison out of the fruit and transforms the fruit of the tree into an elixir which spiritually awakens the one partaking of it.

This is analogous to the spiritual journey of seeking the pure truth—a process where the soul slowly begins relinquishing all attachments to and identifications with the false self and the illusionary world. What is left, after the process of surrendering the illusion is complete, is the knowing of the truth of who we truly are and of our sacred Oneness with all that is. This is the alchemical process of dissolving illusion into the pure elixir of light, which is pure love. Even though this is a process of renouncing something that never existed, the elixir resulting from the journey adds to the expansion of the infinite library and consciousness of God, which is us.

We can see the greater truth of the oneness of all things scientifically in the hologram. If we were to take a tiny piece of a hologram, called a "fractal," and kept breaking it down to tinier and tinier pieces, which a scientist could do ad infinitum, without coming to an end, he would still find that each tiny fractal contains the whole hologram within it. In the same way, everyone in creation contains the full pattern of God within themselves because everyone and everything is God. God is all there is and therefore if we exist then we must be God. I hope this great truth is starting to sink in deeper and deeper into your consciousness. As Jeshua stated in *A Course In Miracles*, the truth can be summed up in two words: **GOD IS**. When a person's spiritual development is fully complete, she will see and experience infinite Love and Joy that will never end and will continue to become greater and greater throughout infinity.

In meditation I was shown very clearly that every cell in my body was in the process of being transformed into God Consciousness. I not only saw this, I experienced the feeling of my cells going through this metamorphosis. Previously, I had been shown in numerous ways and told that the God Gene had exploded in me, which seemed to be confirmed through this meditation. Throughout my spiritual evolution there have been times I felt quite alone in my process, yet at each of those junctures, there was an intersession through revelations, indicating my light, my purpose, my spiritual potential and more.

I am writing this book in a time in which the conflict between those of the light and those entrapped in darkness is becoming more and more intense. What is written here is how to break free of the most insidious matrix of all, which is our identification with the individual ego. It is important to begin this journey of enlightenment, which will eventually free us of all illusion, darkness and limitation. If this is what you seek, then I hope this book will be a great light for you.

Reflection One

I speak of my experience of dissolving the ego and moving into Union with God. It is not necessary and it may not even be appropriate in this incarnation for you to take the final step into that Union. My intent for you, in reading this book, is to consider the possibility of reaching this state of who you truly are. You have the opportunity to begin planting the seeds within this present incarnation that will eventually lead your soul to this Blissful Union.

Two

Who Is God?

This is an extremely important chapter in your understanding of the great realization of who you truly are. I have already mentioned many times the fact that we are God and yet, repetition is necessary to allow the consciousness to slowly begin the acceptance and embodiment of this great and holy Truth.

The question of who God is has been debated and taught in varying religions with many different concepts of what God is. I now want to share a truth of who and what God is to you. The subject that I will now write about in the next two paragraphs, in my own words, is partially from a book, *A Course of Love*, which was dictated by Jeshua to a woman named Mari Perron many years after Jeshua had dictated the book, *A Course in Miracles*. In order to fully understand and accept what I am about to write, a soul would need to accept the one premise that I speak about in this book, which is that each one of us is God. God is in everyone and everything that exists. **There is only God and nothing else exists but God.**

We all have spiritual gifts and one of the strongest gifts I've always had is the Acceptance and Understanding of Truth. Right from the beginning of my spiritual journey, it was very easy for me to realize and accept the great truth of who we truly are and our Oneness with God. I never thought much about it because it was such a natural part of who I am. It also came naturally for me to be able to separate spiritual truths from fiction. The gift or gifts each of us have, kind of like a Superpower if you will, can aid us on our journey through life. A person might have the gift of Patience, in which he receives just about everything that happens in life in peace and acceptance. Patience is a doorway to God. It is a virtue that allows a spiritual seeker to see things in a clear light without all the distortion that reaction brings forth. Patience brings peace to a person regardless of what is happening in the outer world and eventually leads to spiritual awakening.

Another person might have the gift of Forgiveness so that whatever another does against her, she is able to move into a process of forgiving the other person and letting go of the situation without any resentment. Forgiveness can be one of the most difficult virtues to manifest as it usually requires letting go of some act you feel was done against you in anger or spite. This virtue can awaken one to deeper levels of Compassion, another Superpower. Other virtues such as Peace, Joy and Gratitude can also awaken a person and place them on the glorious path toward Union with God.

Find your gift or gifts you are most familiar and confident with and use them to pave the path toward spiritual awakening. This awakening will lead you face to face with the fact that you and God are one and the same. There is no greater Truth than This.

In the book *A Course of Love*, it is stated that whatever you believe about yourself and life in general is who God is to you. **The truth is that God is Infinite Unconditional Love without individuality or separate attributes. Love simply is, without any other traits.** When God created us, we were still a part of God with the consciousness of Pure Love. Each soul had a uniqueness different from every other soul. This uniqueness, along with the free will bestowed on each soul by our Creator, opened the door to infinite possibilities. At some point, with the power of free will, we chose to seemingly separate ourselves from God, which allowed us to create an illusionary world in which we are able to create a version of our own God in whatever way our free will chose. **So, since we are God, the belief of who we think we are is the God we have created.** Do you get the significance of that last statement?

You can look at it in this way: Love is the canvas on which our belief system and thoughts paint our own unique version of God. Our free will is the paintbrush we use to create our painting of God. There is no judgment as to what we create with our free will, we just have to realize that, in this illusion, we and we alone experience the effects of our own creations. The law of cause and effect is life's mirror back to us, of our beliefs and actions that manifest in our lives.

This law eventually helps to awaken the soul to a realization that the only thing that will bring us true joy and peace is to come into attunement with our true nature of God, which is Pure Unconditional Love.

This is important information in the understanding of what God is to each of us, so I will repeat it in a slightly different way. With free will, we are able to superimpose our beliefs and actions on the fabric of Love to give it uniqueness, sort of like taking a piece of clay and molding it into whatever form we desire. We are God and our thoughts have unlimited power, so if we believe in limitation, which just about everybody on Earth does, then the God we are creating is a God of limitation. If we believe in hatred, then our God is a God of hatred. If we believe in peace, then our God is a God of Peace. If we are fearful, then our God is a God of fear. If we believe in Pure Unconditional Love, then our God is a God of Unconditional Love.

Whatever you believe about yourself, others, and life in general constitutes your personal belief of who God is.

If this sounds strange to us, it just means that there are many concepts and limiting beliefs that are keeping us from finding the truth. I accept that this book will help a person to open and expand into greater possibilities. As a soul starts to come into a realization of who they truly are, they will realize the Truth, which will set a soul free. Also, as a soul advances on this spiritual journey, they will come to the full realization that God is Pure Unconditional Love. One way to begin to embody deeper truths is by reflecting on one's spiritual realizations and awakenings, while holding those experiences in mind for longer and longer periods of time.

Are you saying that each one of us has created our own version of God and this is our own particular God?

Yes, but if the God that was created by a soul is not based on Pure Unconditional Love, then it is a false god that can actually never exist since LOVE IS ALL THERE IS. This false self that you may believe you are will never fulfill you, no matter how much money or material possessions you have. We were born in Pure Love and this is the only thing that will fulfill us. Through free will and our desire to experience life separate from God, which is impossible, we fell into a deep sleep and in this dream world we are creating our own version of what God is. Eventually, all souls will awaken into a realization that we are and always have been God. In the distant past, a person would have been put to death for such blaspheme as to even suggest that we are God. Just think of how many different versions of God we have created in this world and in the physical universe as Earth is definitely not the only planet with sentient life on it (this world is defined as a life form that has the ability to raise its consciousness by its own efforts, or that of Grace). This third dimension is also not the only dimension as there are infinite dimensions and universes. This is the glory of God's Creation, which will continually expand throughout infinity.

In the process of each of us creating our own God, it is as if we have created a unique painting of God which, in a sense, will rule our lives according to that projection we have created. There is only one true painting or projection that will open the door into the Kingdom of Heaven and that is one made of Pure Unconditional Love, which is our true nature. When a soul reaches this state of development, a soul will realize that they are God in a physical body manifesting on Earth for a certain purpose. Jeshua and other great spiritual beings manifested this Oneness with God. When a soul on their spiritual journey on Earth finally reaches this state of full spiritual development, they will only act out of Pure Love.

I will let you know how I perceive God. God, to me, is the Oneness of all that is through all universes and dimensions, all time and space without end, continually expanding forever throughout eternity. My God is Pure Unconditional Love, Pure and Holy Innocence, Infinite Mind totally conscious of all that is since It is all that is. My God is Infinite Joy, Peace, Light, Beauty, Creativeness, Power and Grace in Divine Relationship with all my brothers and sisters. All of this is who God is to me and more and thus who I perceive myself to truly be. I perceive that this great final awakening will happen when a soul has voluntarily relinquished all identification with and attachment to the illusionary being which they thought they were. In this full realization of their Union with God, that soul will continue to grow and expand, becoming more and more joyous and creative throughout all eternity without end.

When a soul reaches a state of full awakened consciousness, he or she will fully realize his Union with God. Don't worry that you will have to reach this state before you are ready to enter Heaven. There are many levels of Heaven a soul will encounter on the way to Union with God. In the realm of time, it took us eons to get to this low level of consciousness from our original Holy State. Over eons, we as souls have been working our way back to the Union with God. I pray and accept that there are many on Earth at this time who are open to embodying this truth.

The majority of souls on Earth will gradually advance through many different levels of consciousness, or dimensions, before the full Union with God takes place. The physical Earth, at this time, is right on the precipice of expanding from the third dimension into the fifth dimension. The fifth dimension will be like heaven compared to the lower third dimension. This is an opportunity that has come around again after many thousands of years and there are many souls who have been preparing themselves for this glorious event. Are you starting to get a slight glimpse of the great reality of who we truly are and the infinite Joy and Love, which is our true nature? This is not a philosophy or religion but the sacred truth of who we are. This truth awaits us if we are willing to let go of this illusion. That truly is all we have to do. This can be done at whatever pace we want. We don't have to become a saint, we are God. We simply have to renounce and release this illusionary world and egoic self. The majority on Earth may have difficulty conceiving of this, yet at some point in their spiritual journey they will reach the point of not only conceiving it, but also becoming it. Also know that the path does not need to be a path of sacrifice and pain. God does not want sacrifice, She only wants us to wake up to the unimaginable love and joy that awaits us for all eternity.

A soul does not need to reach the state of Pure Unconditional Love before being freed from this dream of illusion, although awakening from illusion automatically brings one into a state of Pure Unconditional Love. That is our true nature. What is required is the renouncing and releasing of all identification with the false self. I have shared this truth many times as this is the basis and foundation of the path to enlightenment. It is not an easy path as it is literally the death of our ego, which unfortunately most people believe they are. We are dying to something that never existed.

Your spiritual evolution will bring you to the realization that **YOU ARE GREATER THAN YOU CAN EVER BEGIN TO IMAGINE.**

The process of relinquishing the ego that I am writing about can be a shortcut to awakening to this great reality. As I mentioned, it is not an easy path, and this journey is usually not even contemplated until a soul reaches a certain level of spiritual development. It can be accomplished by a soul who is totally determined to free themselves from this illusionary world. When Jeshua walked the earth, he made the statement: **"He who would give up his life will find life"** (Matthew 16:25). The life Jeshua was teaching us to let go of is the false ego. This is the great key to freedom. The chapter on the ego will give you greater insight into this process.

You say we are God, then what is the soul and how did it come into being?

There is no time in reality, but because I need to put this into words, I will say that: In the beginning there was God or Infinite Love. Where did God come from? God always was and will always be. God is Love and Love desired companionship, so God created the soul, which is the individuation of God into many unique individuals, using the essence of God Himself to create these souls. Each soul was given free will, otherwise they could not be the companion that God desired. Free will allowed the soul to fully discover and create whatever it chose. Each soul is unique from every other soul, with a special awareness of who they are, which could be called: I AM THAT I AM. With free will, the soul eventually had the desire to experience life separate from God without the guidance of God, sort of like an adolescent wanting to experience life on their own without the input of their parents. Of course, this separation from God is impossible, since God is all there is, but because the soul was created with all the power of God, the impossible seemed to come into being...and I stress the word "seemed." The whole physical universe is a holographic projection of this "impossibility." In order to experience separation from God, we fell into a deep sleep in which we are dreaming that we are separate from God. It is an illusion since nothing can be separate from all that is, God. It was through fear that we believed we had actually separated from God. It was through this fearful thought that the nonexistent entity called the "ego" seemed to come into being. The ego was seemingly birthed through fear, which is the opposite of Love.

That is how powerful we are as God: that we were able to create the impossible. Unfortunately, through eons of time, we became more and more identified with this illusion and the egoic self, that we seem to suffer and die. Thankfully, we are in a time of great awakening in which many are waking up and realizing that Love is the only thing that can bring us joy. We are not who this world teaches us we are. **We are God and we are greater than we could ever imagine. This is the truth that will set us free.**

How does a person perceive of and embody the idea of God and infinity?

This cannot be perceived or embodied while there is still a belief in and attachment to the egoic self. I remember the first time that I experienced the infinity of mind without boundaries and with no trace of Gil; he didn't exist. At that time, the experience was almost a little scary because of the lack of boundaries and the loss of identification with the individual I thought I was. Now this truth is a permanent knowing in my consciousness.

What I am saying throughout this text will be like a seed planted in the minds of those who are in any way open to this truth. This seed will come to fruition according to the will and state of consciousness of the individual who receives it. There are some now walking the earth who are ready to accept this truth and embody it fully. Be patient with yourself and continue to observe the person you believe you are until your constant practice of **impersonal self-observation** dissolves the illusion and unites you with the unimaginable truth of who you truly are. I will speak more about the method of impersonal self-observation later.

In this illusionary world, when a person is put in a position of great power, most will become more egotistical and prideful. When a soul starts to experience the unimaginable glory of who they are with no limitations whatsoever, that soul becomes more and more humble through the experience of this great realization. This is truly the only journey that will totally fulfill a soul completely. Many Blessings on this journey.

Reflection Two

In this chapter, I give an example of who God is to me. I also outline how our experiences, beliefs and consciousness create our reality of what God is to us. This is a truth that I invite you to contemplate very deeply. The question is, are we satisfied with the God we have created? If not, you might want to start contemplating what kind of God you would really feel comfortable with. I invite you to begin studying the lives of great beings such as Jeshua, Buddha, St. Francis and those who embodied a potent relationship with God. Begin this divine journey of opening the door into the nature of what God is to you. God is the Supreme Consciousness that sustains the universe. God is and always will be One with everything that ever existed in reality. Start creating this relationship by living your life in accordance with what is true for you.

Three

The Early Journey

I want to give you a little insight into the path that I traveled on my journey into Christ Consciousness. I am hoping that in reading about my life it will help you on your journey.

My personal journey in this lifetime was definitely not a bed of roses as I suffered deeply on so many levels. I was born on November 19, 1941, in the mountains of New Mexico in a little town called Park View. I was born into a very large family with thirteen children. I do not remember much about the first four years of my life except that I had the feeling at the age of three or four that I could do anything. I was a very bold and confident child. In those early years, I also had the sense that I had to be perfect. My need to be perfect followed me for a good portion of my life until I realized the futility of this striving. I realized the person I believed I was, who was striving for perfection, was an illusion itself. With this understanding I began observing the one I had been identified with all my life and his striving for perfection. I started withdrawing my identity from this façade by observing what it was doing without any identification with it. Through my witness observations, I fully began my journey of giving up the illusion of the person I thought I was, as well as the illusion of this world. This surrender opened the door to a path that led to God. I have since realized that my striving for perfection was an illusion because we are always expanding and gaining new experiences, as is God, for we are One.

Our family was poor, but I think the early years of my life were mainly happy. My life changed drastically when I was four years old. My mom died shortly after giving birth to her thirteenth child, my youngest sister. It was at this time that my whole world was turned upside down. A few days before her death, my dad took my younger brother and me to stay with relatives in New Mexico in order to give my mom a chance to rest and recuperate after having given birth. My dad got a phone call a couple of days later informing him that Mom had been taken to the hospital. He flew back to California to be with her. She passed on before he got there. My younger brother and I never even got a chance to go to the funeral. We were immediately sent to an orphanage for boys in Albuquerque. The orphanage was run by Catholic nuns. Many of the nuns in the orphanage were very cruel and some were even sadistic. The nun who was directly in charge of us was particularly cruel and seemed to single me out when something went wrong.

The loss of my mom, dad, and family at that young age really stunted my emotional development. The punishments and beatings handed out by the nuns and their doctrine of sin and guilt, which were daily drummed into our heads, did not help the situation. The orphanage was definitely not a place for a child to develop a healthy emotional system. The death of my mom and my experience in the orphanage left me a very emotionally and mentally confused, angry young boy. After five years in the orphanage, my dad was finally able to bring us home. By that time, I had erected an impenetrable protective shield around myself and as a result I had a hard time bonding with my dad and siblings.

Before I had fully created the protective shield around myself, I was given a glimpse of who I am. In the orphanage, we were not allowed to have any money. If a relative happened to send a child some money, the nuns would intercept it and keep it. One day on the playground, I was with my brother and a friend and without thinking, I said that I was going to find some money. I then pointed to a spot on the ground and said, "There is a dime." I swept back the dirt from that spot and there was a dime. I then walked over to another spot and said, "There is a quarter." I again swept back the dirt and there was a quarter. I did this several times and each time there was the exact coin denomination at the exact spot where I said it would be. Back then, I was either five or six years old and didn't think much about it. It seemed natural to me that the coins should be where I said they would be. It wasn't until much later that I realized the rarity of what had actually happened.

I do not feel any judgment toward anyone regarding my experience in the orphanage because I know that before I came into Earth, I chose to go through these experiences for a spiritual purpose. When we begin to understand that we as souls choose certain lessons to aid in our spiritual evolution, it will be much easier to let go of the idea that we are a victim. Then we can heal all the anger, blame and judgments that are part of the victim identity. The victim identity is a huge hurdle to heal on the path to spiritual awakening.

As I grew older, my insecurity and anger prevented me from really opening up to anybody. Even though I had friends, I usually had a feeling of being isolated and of not fitting in. Even the girlfriends I had were unable to penetrate my defenses. The only time I felt like I belonged was when I was playing sports because I usually did well in athletics, and sports did not require intimate communication.

Because the military draft was in effect at the time I graduated high school, I joined the army right after graduation and spent three years in Japan.

I got out of the army in the spring of 1962. For the next six years I was pretty much caught up in the illusions of this world. Like most people, I was trying to make as much money as I could and was always looking for that perfect girl who would make my life complete. During three of those years, I was heavily involved in gambling by playing the horses and cards. Thankfully, the illusionary dream I was having would soon be brought into the Light, allowing me to experience the Truth of who I truly am.

There are generally four stages that a soul will go through on their way to enlightenment. The first stage is one in which the soul starts to feel that the life they are leading is unfulfilling and unsatisfying. He or she realizes that there is something very important missing in their lives and this is when the searching for that something begins. He or she may not even know what that something is but the restlessness and the prodding from within cannot be ignored. This inner prodding eventually leads the soul on a search for something to fulfill their lives. Stage one led me on a spiritual search for truth, which completely changed the direction of my life and the way that I perceived life.

Stage two of my spiritual journey began in 1967. This is a stage in which a person is introduced, in a myriad of ways, to perceiving life in a very different way. At that time, my younger brother introduced me to marijuana and a little later on to LSD. I resisted at first, but because some of my friends were willing to take the plunge, I tried it also. The effect that these drugs had on me was to awaken a very strong longing for God deep inside myself, which caused me to totally reevaluate my life. This simply helped to awaken me to the truth that there was much more to life than what we perceive with the five senses.

The process I experienced of preparing myself for spiritual enlightenment was a very long and difficult one. Fortunately, in this day and age, we are living in unprecedented times of greater light and consciousness on Earth right now, and the spiritual path is much easier to find and walk for those who are seeking truth. Each of us has a very unique path to travel and if we are sincere about knowing the truth, everything we need will be provided.

Shortly after my mind-altering spiritual experiences, I quit the job I had in the tech industry and pretty much dropped out of society, as the term was used back in the 1960s. For the next two years, I became more and more of a loner because the outer world no longer held much of an attraction for me. While my friends continued to party, I spent most of the time alone contemplating the reality of God and my relationship to Him. I would often walk to a park near our apartment and sit under a weeping willow tree and contemplate spiritual truths and my new direction in life. During parts of those two years, I lived in my station wagon while I tried to understand the purpose of my life. I devoured every spiritual book I could get my hands on. I was, at that time, especially drawn to the metaphysical information that came through the readings given by Edgar Cayce. I even gave talks at the high school I had attended on Edgar Cayce.

In 1969, the direction of my life changed dramatically because of an experience I had. On a very beautiful spring day, I drove up to some hills in Northern California to get away from the city and to contemplate my new direction in life. I climbed up to the top of one of the hills and rested under a tree beside a stream. I was looking up at the sky when all of a sudden, a huge vision of Jeshua (Jesus the Christ) appeared above me. His arms were to the side with his palms opened. I felt myself leave my body and float up to where Jeshua was, and we began to talk. I am not conscious of what was said, except for a comment he made about my body. When he said this, I looked down and saw my body lying beneath the tree. I don't know how long our conversation lasted before I floated back into my body. When I reentered my body, a question immediately arose in my mind: **"What is God?"** The answer from within was immediate and the voice I heard was the most beautiful, yet authoritative I had ever heard: **"God is Mind in Space."** I will never forget that voice or those words.

After a short time, I got up and started walking on one of the many trails that marked the hill. As I walked, I heard the same inner voice talking to me about the spiritual path. In essence, the voice told me that I would encounter many things on my spiritual journey that would appear to be good and right, but to remain simple and I would reach my destination.

Shortly after that experience on the hills of Northern California, I came to the conclusion that I was on Earth for a purpose and that I had better get back into the flow of life until that purpose was revealed to me. I signed up for college in the summer of 1969. Two weeks before my first day of college I received a pamphlet in the mail from somebody who attended the same high school I did. I did not know the person who sent it very well and so it was curious that he would send it to me. I don't even know how he got my mailing address! The pamphlet was about a spiritual group called the Holy Order of MANS. There were also many women in the Order as the term "MANS" is an acronym for the striving of the members. The Order was started through a revelation from Jeshua to the head of the Order, Father Paul, who was a very highly evolved spiritual master. Their main headquarters was in San Francisco, about twenty minutes from where I was living at the time. The pamphlet intrigued me because their teachings were not based on Western religious doctrine, but had more of an Eastern mystical and metaphysical flavor. I wanted to find out more about this Order, so a few days before I was to start college, I decided to take a drive to San Francisco and talk to somebody at the Order house to find out more about the organization and their purpose.

When I arrived at the main Order house, a priest was summoned to talk to me about their purpose and to answer any questions I had. While talking to the priest, I intuitively knew that this was where I was supposed to be at that time. While the priest was speaking to me, my mind came up with many reasons why I could not join this organization, but intuitively I knew my rationalizations would be of no avail. I knew this was where I was supposed to be at that time. I moved into the Holy Order of MANS' main house in San Francisco that very day. It was an abrupt and total severing of my old way of life.

My entrance into the Order was the beginning of stage three for me. This is a stage of testing, transforming, and the beginning of dissolving the false ego. Stage three was by far the most difficult period of my life. In many cases, this stage is considered an initiation and will test a spiritual aspirant as to how much he really wants the truth. Generally speaking, seekers will go through this period on many different levels of difficulties and testing depending on the development of the soul and the purpose for which the soul came to Earth.

I write about the fourth stage in upcoming chapters as well as continuing to discuss in further detail about the first three stages of a person's spiritual journey.

Reflection Three

Throughout this chapter I talk about my spiritual journey and how it led me to a greater level of merging with God. I share the first three stages out of four in which I began the process of dissolving the illusionary self I believed I was. We are all so very different and our journeys are unique. If you are ready to seek the truth in earnest, this understanding will be foremost in your heart and mind. I invite you to observe your spiritual path and contemplate these first three stages and where you are on the journey.

Four

The Ego

One of the spiritual tools that is being used more and more in this day and age is the removal of entities from people, homes, and other areas of life. There are many all over the world who are performing this service. The most profound entity removal, or exorcism, is the removal or dissolution of the false ego that we believe we are. This exorcism must be done mainly by the individual himself. The ego is the greatest source of deception in this illusion. Also, the ego is the most difficult and illusive entity to remove. To the individual, the removal of the ego is like an act of suicide as this is the removal of who we falsely believe we are. In preparation for this transformation, a person must have a very clear understanding of what the ego is. The ego is the only barrier between God and us.

The ego is a necessary part of our lessons and growth in this realm of illusion. There is nothing wrong with having an ego. In this book I am addressing those who are seeking and ready to transcend their illusionary ego. As a soul becomes more awakened, the path of dissolving the ego becomes clearer. There is absolutely no judgment as to how a soul chooses to live their life. The question that each one must answer is whether he or she wants to continue experiencing pain and separation or Divine Love, Bliss, Peace and much, much more.

The ego in itself is not bad in that it really has no existence except through our false belief that it is who we are. It is our identification with it that gives it all its power. Our identification with the ego gives it the power to control our lives. The more we identify with it, the more it becomes a little dictator. The false ego created the illusion of the physical world and the individual, which most people think that they are. If we did not have an ego, we would not be able to individualize. An analogy that might give you a clearer picture of the ego is to imagine the sun, which shines upon the earth. The light of the sun is not individualized but simply shines all over. Now, if we took a magnifying glass and allowed the light of the sun to shine through the glass, we are able to focus the sunlight. We are, in a sense, individualizing part of it. In the same way, our true consciousness is infinite. Through the ego, we are seemingly able to individualize ourselves in order to experience the illusion of life separate from the Oneness of God, which, of course, is impossible since God is all there is.

Continuing with this analogy, the light of the sun can be focused to burn down a house, or to bring us warmth on a cold day. In the same way, how we use our will and how we choose to focus it determines whether it brings us happiness or misery. An unbalanced ego will burn the house down, whereas a balanced ego will spread warmth and love wherever she goes. **Our purpose on the spiritual path is to relinquish the false ego so that God's Will, which is Love, can be focused through us.**

The false ego can be likened to a guest who we invite into our house. This guest immediately begins to start wrecking the furniture and making a mess everywhere he goes in the house. He then starts insulting you every time he sees you and begins stealing your valuables. He also insults any of your friends who come over. You now realize how dangerous he is and begin to fear him. You become afraid that if you ask him to leave, he will harm you. He becomes so entrenched in your whole life that you forget how nice your life was before you invited him into your house. You begin to live in fear, not knowing what he is going to do next.

How many of us would put up with a guest in our house who is threatening and criticizing us and our friends? I don't think any of us would consciously invite such a guest into our home. What if I were to tell you that each one of us, with the exception of those who have transcended the illusory self, has a visitor living with us twenty-four hours a day, who is even worse than the unwanted guest? At least the so-called "guest" would be obvious in his negative actions and demeanor and we would ask him to leave. Our internal guest is so subtle and cunning, that it is almost impossible to detect its presence. In fact, this visitor is so devious that it makes us believe that we are who it is. It causes us to believe that we want exactly what it desires, even though, in most cases, it is the exact opposite of what we truly want. From the moment of its seeming inception, the false ego is the guest that has been leading us down a path of pain and despair.

Where is this illusive entity, called the ego, located? **The ego is a state of mind, a mental identification with a false belief system.** If we believe in lack and limitation, we are being controlled by the mind of the ego. The desire to separate ourselves from God brought the false ego into existence. The ego lives in the belief that we are separate from each other. If we believe in judgment, we are supporting one of the pillars of the ego. Our belief in death as a reality perpetuates the ego. Some of the most powerful tools of deception that the ego has at its disposal are sin, guilt, and fear. We can list any negative or limiting belief or attitude that we have and we are looking directly at one of the mental pillars of the ego. When we honestly look at these beliefs in ourselves, we can see how deeply ingrained some of them are. The majority of people on Earth are totally identified with these beliefs. We assume that negativity and limitations are a natural part of life and don't even question their authenticity. That is why the ego has had its way in this world for so long.

Most of our religions have doctrines that say we are limited, sinful creatures and we should repent for our sins. Unfortunately, some religious institutions are fortresses of the ego and have done more harm than good when it comes to revealing truth. Jeshua spoke of the scribes and the Pharisees and how they had access to the sacred teachings, which could free a soul from illusion, but would not follow the teachings and would prevent the people from having access to this knowledge. If the Pure Truth was taught to the masses, this would be a very different world as we would realize that the holy altar is within each of our hearts. True worship takes place in the privacy of our minds and hearts as God is within us, and we are One with God.

There is only One thing that is in existence and that is God. I repeat this truth many times throughout this book in many different ways because it is the essence of Truth that needs to be embodied.

In many organized religions there is a reconfirmation that we are sinners and deserve to be punished. Many religions who preach sin and guilt are trapped in that belief system throughout their lives. Even so, many of these religions perform a positive service for many. Jeshua told his disciples that he had many more things to tell them, but at that time they were unable to hear or understand what he had to say. So he spoke to them on the level they were able to comprehend. We are in a very exciting time on Earth where many people across the world are now able to hear and understand the Truth that will set them free. Souls are spiritually awakening at a speed that has never happened before in the history of mankind.

The ego will do everything in its power to keep us asleep. To know the truth is the last thing the ego wants for us, because Truth is the Light that reveals to a soul that darkness never existed and that only God is. This elimination of darkness obliterates the ego, which can only exist in illusion or darkness. The ego seemed to come into being out of darkness and cannot endure the Light of Truth. **The only thing that gives the ego life is our belief that it is who we are.** Once we start opening up to the Light, all our false beliefs begin to disappear. When the ego finally dissolves into the nothingness from whence it came, we are reborn into the Light and into our Union with God.

What if some of our beliefs are really true, so why should we let go of them?

Let me assure you that anything that is true will remain after a person goes through the transformation. It is impossible for truth to be destroyed. It is our false beliefs and identifications that have created all our fears, pains, division, and unhappiness. **In reality, what we are giving up is nothing in exchange for everything.** If a person really understood the magnitude of that last statement, he would immediately begin to search for the Truth that will set him free. There would be no price too big to pay. As I shared in Chapter 2, Jeshua put it in another way when he said, "He who would give up his life, will find life" (Matthew 16:25). The life Jeshua is asking us to give up is the false, limited, and painful life that the ego has seemingly created, which most people identify with completely. A spiritually awakened person would obviously give up that which prevents them from experiencing their true nature of Pure Unconditional Love and Innocence.

Most spiritual students have heard of the "Dark Night of the Soul." My journey through the third stage of letting go of my false ego consisted of many of these dark periods. All the concepts of who I thought I was and which I had reinforced over many years of habitual reactions were totally challenged by the Light of Truth that started to penetrate my belief system in 1969. These challenges were vehemently resisted by the ego. The conflict that was going on between the ego and the light created some very intense discomfort in my physical, emotional, and mental bodies. Had it not been for my total desire to fulfill God's Will, there is no way I would have continued on the path that I was traveling. It doesn't mean I would have given up my spiritual journey, it just means I would have tried to find an easier path back to God. Eventually though, if I were seeking true liberation, I would, at some point, have needed to face and dissolve the ego regardless of what path I chose. We must face our own darkness in order to move into the light. The greater the darkness we face, the greater the light will be when we wake up.

How do we give up the false ego that we believe we are?

First of all, we must have a desire to know the truth more than anything else. If we don't have this overwhelming desire to know who we really are, we are defeated before we begin the journey. My desire to fulfill God's Will was the engine that propelled me on my path. Our desire to know the truth, above all else, will allow us to honestly assess our current situation without judgment or condemnation. We have to look into all the corners and dark recesses of our mind to understand what has been driving us. In order to see more clearly, we need more spiritual light. The process of letting go of our false beliefs and receiving more light happens simultaneously. If we detect that we have a lot of resentment against someone, we must observe the resentment without any identification with the thought. Through **impersonal self-observation**, or what many know as **witnessing**, we begin the process of disconnecting our attachments to the false beliefs that keep us from the Divine Light that we all seek. Make a sincere effort to understand that any resentment we have is simply the egoic mind trying its best to keep us believing in the illusion. Everything we experience is happening in our own mind. It is our dream and our dream only. Eventually, we will realize that resentment, or any other negative or limited idea, comes from a false belief of who we are. The foundation of this false belief is based on the belief that we are separate from God and from others. I cannot overestimate the importance of this understanding.

All we need at the beginning is a little willingness, which will lead to greater willingness, which will eventually lead us to the final step of awakening from this dream of illusion. The great benefit of taking our first small step is that we will receive as much help in this process as we can accept. **Remember: this whole process is taking place in our mind. We need to live and think the truth as much as possible.** The transformation process will bring about a new perception of our self and others. Our physical and material conditions may not necessarily change that much, but our outlook and attitude will be totally transformed.

Let me give you an analogy of what is taking place in this process. Imagine that you are in a large, cluttered room that is completely dark, and you keep bumping into the debris that fills the room and you continually hurt yourself. You are aware that you have to clean up this room if you want to stop hurting yourself. You cannot see because of the darkness, but you can feel all the junk in the room because you keep stumbling into it wherever you turn. You have no idea where you can put all the clutter, but you decide that you must begin somewhere. You begin moving the debris to one side of the room in hopes of there being a door or window that will allow some light into the room so you can see. You move a few pieces of junk to one side, and to your amazement, you see a tiny shaft of light coming from the area in which you have been clearing. Having seen this first glimmer of light gives you hope and inspiration to clean up more of the clutter. As you clear more of the junk, more light fills the room until you notice a doorway that had been covered up by all the clutter. You also get the sense of invisible helpers who were assisting you in this process. When you finally open the door, you see a world outside that is more beautiful than you could have ever imagined. You are now free to walk out into the sunlight into a world of infinite beauty and joy.

The junk in the room represents our false beliefs, identifications, and desires of the ego. Moving the debris in the dark represents the beginning of our willingness to let go of some of our false beliefs. The light beaming into the room represents our own inner light, which naturally shines as we are willing to truthfully face ourselves and begin letting go of our limited and destructive beliefs. The invisible helpers are your spiritual guides and angels who want to assist us in finding truth. The door into the outside world represents a state of spiritual awakening a person experiences as a result of dissolving their false identity. This spiritual awakening leads to an inner experience of complete peace and contentment.

The journey into Christ Consciousness necessitates that we recognize that darkness is the other half of light. Our focus must be on that which underlies both. We must be the awareness that observes all that is taking place, without judgment or identification with either. We will realize that any judgment is a roadblock to embodying the great Light that we are.

What is the best way to let go of all judgment?

By observing all that is happening in a totally impersonal way. Simply be the observer without the concept of identification, right or wrong, good or bad. This process will eventually lead to the dissolution of the ego and the freedom of the Spirit that each one of us truly is. **The main question we have to ask ourselves is: how willing are we to let go of our identification with the ego and the life we have believed we have been living all our life?** That is the question each soul will have to eventually answer in the affirmative if they desire spiritual freedom.

As we take on more light, we will be filled with compassion as we observe the darkness others are subjected to, but we do not judge those who are committing the offenses. The light that we carry as enlightened beings is a strong beacon to all who are open to receiving it. Each person is their own creator and must make the decision as to when they choose to follow the light. We can be a great light in the world, but we cannot force others to follow the light. This is because of the gift of free will that our Creator has bestowed upon each one of us. A soul can choose to remain asleep as long as they desire, with no judgment from God, but they will have to continually experience the negative effects created by the ego until they are finally ready to let go of the illusion.

It is impossible to understand truth if we don't first dissolve some of our false beliefs that block the Light of Truth from reaching our awareness. Jeshua said, "Seek and you shall find" (Matthew 7:7). Our seeking for truth is the beginning of this effort. There will come a time in a person's spiritual development when he or she will even have to give up seeking. I will go into more detail on this idea in a later chapter.

The ego comes in all forms, shapes, and appearances and can appear as timid, angry, sad, happy, loving, and confident. Now, being happy, loving, and confident may seem like attractive traits, but if these attributes are supported by the belief that we are the ego, it is only a fragile façade as there is no real joy behind these façades. There is actually a great deal of fear behind these false façades. The exterior façade of love and joy that the ego projects can be overshadowed at any moment by the fear that lurks underneath, for the ego is the manifestation of fear.

I grew up with a very big chip on my shoulder because of the loss of my mom and the feeling of being rejected by my dad. The harsh treatment I was subjected to in the orphanage also played a big role in creating a very insecure and angry personality. After my dad took me out of the orphanage at age ten, I became a person who was ready to fight at the drop of a hat. I got in many fights throughout high school because of all the pent-up anger due to my childhood experiences. Because of all my insecurities, it was very, very difficult for me not to react to others if I perceived even the slightest judgment or offense against me.

There was a time in my early twenties when I was so afraid of my own ego, because of the control it had over me, that I had to think twice before going to parties because I was concerned that if somebody did or said something I did not like, my ego would cause me to get in a fight. I did not like to get into brawls, but because of the big insecure ego I had at the time, I was not really in control. The ego was in total command of my personality and my life at that time. The ego totally conceals the truth that we are God.

Fear is a big part of a person's life when the ego is in control. The reason for this is that if we are not spiritually awake, we are living in darkness and **one of the principal attributes of darkness is fear,** regardless of how well it is hidden from others or from ourselves. **In this world, the ego is synonymous with a person's identity.** The ego has lived its whole life through us, yet most people don't have the faintest idea that this ego wants full dominion over us. The ego is aware that in reality, it has no existence. It also knows that our true nature is eternal, and it feels that if it can dominate us, then maybe it can steal our eternal nature. The ego is extremely cunning and at the same time totally insane.

I mentioned earlier that the belief in death is one of the most powerful tools the ego has to keep us chained to the illusion of this world. I know it is difficult not to believe in death when death seems to be a natural part of our earthly cycle. I am saying that the realization that death is an illusion becomes a natural part of our knowing as we awaken spiritually. **The only death we must experience to be free is the death of the ego.** When a person has completed the relinquishment of his ego, his physical death will be no more of a trauma than walking from one room into another room of extreme beauty and joy.

The ego will not give up control easily as it has the same self-preservation instinct that any living entity has. It is very aware when a person starts his journey on the spiritual path, and this is when it becomes the most ferocious and cunning. I remember an experience I had many years ago, which will shed some light on this subject. It was during a period when a lot of my emotional baggage from childhood was surfacing. I was at home sitting on the sofa experiencing a lot of mental insecurities, dealing with childhood issues of abandonment and unworthiness. In years past, a mental barrage like this would have sent me into a depressed state, but I just sat there watching my thoughts with no attachment or judgment as to what was taking place in my mind. All of a sudden, my consciousness seemed to be transported to the center of my being where I continued watching my mental process, only then it seemed as if I were in a protective bubble where none of the heavy feelings associated with these thoughts could affect me. From this vantage point I could see very clearly the ego operating through these dark thoughts. As the ego became aware that I was watching and was not being affected by the thoughts, it changed its strategy and started flattering me and telling me how good I was and how I should be proud of myself. Of course, I didn't buy into that either, but it was a great insight into how cunning and illusive the ego can be, because when it can't get you one way, it will try another.

The ego is a master when it comes to deception and it knows all our weaknesses. It doesn't care whether we are suffering, poor, or rich. The ego knows that any of these experiences will most likely keep us asleep and eventually cause us pain, which is the objective of the ego. You might wonder why your own ego would want to cause you misery. The ego maintains its existence through deceiving us into identifying with the joy, success, pain, and misery that seems to be happening in our lives. It wants us to keep believing in this world of illusion because if we stopped believing in the dream, the ego would dissolve into nothingness from whence it came. *Failure* and *Success* are two of the life paths that the ego uses to keep us from discovering our true identity. It is afraid that once we begin questioning things, we will begin to recognize that we are something much more than what it is. This questioning and contemplation of the meaning of life will eventually lead to truth and the dissolution of the ego. So, the ego wants to keep us very busy, either in our misery or in striving to accomplish something special that promises great rewards. Sometimes the attainment of worldly rewards does seem to bring temporary satisfaction, but in time it will never satisfy and will always keep a person striving to get even more.

"Who am I? Where am I going? What is life all about? Is this all there is?" These are the types of questions that come from your True Self. The ego wants no part of these questions. It wants to keep us in the dark, which is the only place it can seemingly exist and continue its deception. The ego must be taken out of the darkness and placed in the light of our consciousness in order to understand and dissolve its false nature.

Do you have any suggestions as to how I might become more aware of my ego? How can I become more aware of my moment-by-moment thought process?

A mountain climber who is making a very difficult climb must be totally aware of his every movement. To lose concentration even for a moment could be fatal. In this same way, if we would practice being the witness to what is happening in our minds without judgment of, or identification with, that experience, we would begin to take control of our thought process, which is a huge step in our awakening. The ego does not like it when we are critiquing our thoughts, because believe it or not, all of the thoughts going through our mind are not our own. We are not even the thinker of those thoughts. Unless a person is spiritually awake, the thoughts he is having are being thought by the ego, which, in reality, does not exist. The ego is the fictional writer of the life script for the majority of people in this world. Most people cannot quiet their minds, even for a few seconds. They do not realize that their identification with all the thoughts running through their minds, which they think are their own thoughts and ideas, are responsible for their so-called "reality." To take control of our lives, we must be aware of and stop identifying with the thoughts, actions, and beliefs that are constantly running through our mind.

Get in the habit of constantly observing your thoughts, without any judgment or interpretation. It is extremely important, so I will repeat that **the practice of observing our thoughts and actions without any identification, judgment, or interpretation is a very powerful way to start unraveling the ego.** Being aware of the thoughts that are passing through our mind without identifying with them will begin the process of releasing the belief and attachment to the false ego.

Spiritual students have been using the practice of **impersonal self-observation** for a long time. There is a good book I read many years ago that really gave me a lot of insight into this practice. It is entitled, *The Mystic Path to Cosmic Power* by Vernon Howard. In the book, Howard's premise refers to the ego as the "false self" of which there are many faces. There are many great books out now that shed light on the subject of the ego. Eckhart Tolle's *The Power of Now* gives the reader great insight into the ego/pain body.

Jeshua's life was the antithesis of the ego. Jeshua took on the mission to display in this third dimension the process a person must go through in order to fully awaken spiritually. This does not mean we have to go through the literal crucifixion, but it does mean we must go through the difficult process of giving up our ego. **The crucifixion was a living symbolic expression of the voluntary relinquishment of the ego.** It is represented in the words, "Not my will, but Yours be done" (Luke 22:42). Jeshua sacrificed his life so that greater spiritual light could enter the world so that his brothers and sisters on Earth could begin to see the Truth. He lived his life as a way of showing us the path to spiritual transformation, which was represented by his resurrection.

Each of us will have to go through this process of relinquishing the ego in our own way. Remember that each person who awakens makes it that much easier for all those who are following on the path to liberation.

Why is that?

We are all part of one mind. When a part of the mind becomes enlightened, it sheds light on the entire mind, which makes it easier for other parts of that same mind to awaken.

There are cases when an individual experiences a sudden awakening through no seemingly spiritual effort of their own in this lifetime. Souls like this have most likely done a lot of spiritual work in past lives, including this lifetime, and are ripe for spiritual awakening when the time presents itself. Spiritual awakenings come in different levels of awareness, depending on the development of the soul having the awakening. A person who reaches *full spiritual development* on Earth would be considered God Realized.

A Christed Being has the power to heal the sick and raise the dead as he is One with God in Consciousness. One such being was Jesus. Other examples of spiritually fully developed beings are Buddha and Krishna. A fully awakened one does only what he is guided to do by the Holy Spirit. His only concern is to help his brothers and sisters who are sincere in their desire to awaken from this dream.

Many may find it difficult to accept that this world is a dream—an illusion—because everything seems so real and substantial. Let's look at this idea in a way we can all relate to. Have you ever had a dream so vivid that you were sure it was actually taking place, only to wake up in the morning to realize it was a dream? I remember when I was about eleven years old, I had a series of dreams that continued from one night to the next like a television series and it seemed so real. One night, the dream ended at a very interesting point and I could not wait to get to bed the next night to see what was going to happen. I have also had vivid dreams in which I had gotten into trouble with the law, and it seemed so real that when I woke up, I was so relieved that I felt like celebrating. It was as if I had actually been given a reprieve from a jail sentence or something even worse.

Yes, but the reason we couldn't distinguish a dream from reality is that we were asleep, we were not conscious.

This is just my point: The great majority of the world is asleep and unaware that they are participating in a holographic vivid dream here on Earth. There is absolutely no judgment in this statement. We have all been asleep and we will all awaken. It is extremely important not to judge another who chooses to take the path of the ego and experience the darker side of life. **Any judgments simply draw us back into the illusion.**

Imagine that you had a favorite sister who had gotten so involved in a television program that when one of the characters on the program died, your sister went into a deep depression. She could not eat or sleep and would not leave the house. Wouldn't you try everything you could think of to wake her out of her misery? You would probably want to shake her and get it into her head that the program is not real and that the characters are only acting. I know this sounds a little far-fetched, but as a person begins the awakening process, he will begin to see right through the illusion which had held him prisoner for many lifetimes. The only reason we cannot awaken from this dream is because of the guilt, fears, and beliefs we think comprise who we are. It is the Light of Truth that will allow us to see the path out of this insane illusion. All true spiritual teachers have come into the world to bear witness to the truth by allowing the Light within them to shine so brightly that it allows those around them to begin to Awaken.

Why do you keep repeating the idea that this world is not real, that it is all a bad dream?

Repetition is absolutely necessary in the process of awakening. We all have lived many dream cycles, which many refer to as "reincarnations." During all these many cycles, we have reinforced our belief in the illusion over and over again. From the day we were born into our current cycle, we have been bombarded twenty-four hours a day with the idea that the world we live in is real. The reason I keep repeating the idea that this world is not real and an illusion, is because it is necessary to reinforce this idea so that this truth can start breaking down all the false concepts, beliefs, and conditioning that this world is true and that we are the illusionary ego.

The way of escape from the ego's world of illusion into reality has been taught by many great teachers. Siddhartha Gautama, who became known as the Buddha after his spiritual awakening, stated that this world is impermanent and that whatever is impermanent is by its very nature illusory (the Sūtra on Impermanence). All things created by God are perfect and eternal. Buddha encouraged his followers to become aware of illusion through correct understanding. The words of these awakened beings are now being understood and practiced by many people in this day and age. Many people around the world are now waking up from this very vivid dream that we have been having.

I want to give you a question to ponder regarding the ego: **Where does the darkness go when the light is turned on?** That's exactly where the ego goes when a person fully wakes up spiritually.

Before I conclude this chapter on the ego, I want to clarify one thing: The ego that I have referred to in this chapter is a fabrication of our false beliefs and has no reality outside the world of illusion. But there is another Ego, one that transcends all limitations, and which knows itself to be glory beyond measure. This is the Ego that comes with the awareness that we are One with God, made in Her image with infinite Power, Joy, Knowledge, Peace and Love. This pure Ego knows that it is holy and perfect in every way and could not be otherwise. The difference between this Ego and the illusionary ego is that the pure Ego does not compare itself with anything or anyone else. How could it compare itself when it knows that everything that is real is One? It is totally aware of the Holy Oneness of all things. **The unbalanced ego is something that was created because of the fear that arose when we believed we had actually separated ourselves from God.** We become more and more aware of our pure Ego as we progress on our spiritual journey. God has created us in Her own image as an extension of Her Self to enjoy and expand the glory of Her unlimited, ever-expanding Creation. This is the amazing truth of who we truly are.

Reflection Four

In this chapter, you can begin to integrate the principles to apply in your life in order to make progress on the path. The ego is the only block toward Full Spiritual Enlightenment. Your sincere desire for the truth will help you to observe the areas in which you are identifying mentally and emotionally with your ego. Observe how real it feels to believe this is who you are; the habitual reactions, becoming identified with your outcomes, questioning why you are the way you are, etc. The ego knows all your weaknesses and has many creative ways to keep you invested in this illusion. Identify how you can use your will to help you have a mental shift, relinquishing the false ego of illusion, step by step. I began this process by observing my reactions to people, situations, and anything that brought forth fear, insecurity, and anger. Through observation, I invite you to meditate and review any situation that causes upset. Integrate impersonal self-observation, not judging the scenario in any way, but just observing how strong the hold in illusion can be.

Five

Unraveling the Ego

Because of the total identification with the ego, the unraveling of it is the most difficult journey a soul will ever have to endure. **It is the dismantling and death of that which we have falsely believed we were.** This transformation is unique to each individual soul. The beginning of this process is what I embarked on from the moment I joined the Holy Order of MANS. In the first year of the Order, I experienced extreme discomfort as a process of dying to the ego unfolded. The thought of leaving the Order was constantly on my mind. There was a consistent burning sensation on the crown of my head, which was extremely uncomfortable. My conditioning of insecurity and anger would take time to unravel.

On my very first morning in the Order during Communion, this message was revealed to me: "Be at peace with yourself and know that the Christ Life will manifest through this being." This was the first of many revelations to come that would give me strength and courage to continue. I was only in the Order for a little over four months when I received word that I would be going out on missionary work. This was highly unusual because I had not even begun missionary classes. Usually, a student would have to go to classes for some time before they were even considered for this work. There were many brothers and sisters who had been taking these classes much longer than I had even been in the Order. At that time, there was a need for someone to go to Lincoln, Nebraska. Father Paul, the head of the Order, asked a Master Teacher to go to the chapel to ask for guidance in choosing the right person to go on this mission. He received word from Spirit that I was the one to go.

Four days before I got word of this transfer to Lincoln, Nebraska, I woke up with the most massive headache I had ever experienced. For three days I laid in bed, unable to get up. I intuitively knew that there were some deep mental patterns in me that were being worked on by my guides in the higher realm. On the fourth day I was finally able to get out of bed. On that day, I was called into Father Paul's office and he told me I would be leaving for Nebraska the very next day.

I left for Lincoln, Nebraska by bus on January 7, 1970. I had never been to the Midwest and had no idea how cold it got there. I left so quickly that I didn't have the chance to gather any warm clothes or even an overcoat. There was one other brother there at the time and he picked me up at the bus station in an old, noisy pickup truck. We drove to the old house where we would be living, which had no insulation whatsoever. There were only a couple of heating vents in the whole house, which put out about as much heat as a few lit matches. It was freezing in the morning when we got up. The two of us would run and stand under one of the vents as we got dressed. This was the beginning of the Holy Order of MANS missionary outreach to different parts of the world.

The nine months I spent in Lincoln were extremely difficult for me because of the constant and continuing daily battle between the ego and my will. In most cases, the darkest hours on our spiritual journey become some of the most important steps in the alchemical process of our spiritual metamorphosis. In early spring of 1970, I was going through an especially dark period and felt that everything I was doing was useless. The thought of leaving the Order continually passed through my mind on a daily basis. On this particular day, I was experiencing a lot of mental and emotional darkness and felt that I was getting nowhere in my spiritual quest. I was sitting on the steps of our mission house in a very dark state when an extremely clear, audible voice said to me, **"Do not use reason to judge your spiritual growth."** Even though the voice did not make me feel any better, at least it assured me that the way I was feeling was not an indication that I was not progressing on the path. I received many beautiful spiritual nuggets from Jeshua. Toward the end of my stay in Nebraska, I had another clear experience with Jeshua when he came to me and said, **"Persist in** your striving and all channels of knowledge and service will be opened to you."** These words were like a healing salve for all the inner turmoil I had been going through in my first year in the Order.

I will relate another experience I had during my second year in the Holy Order of MANS, which will give you some idea of the hold the ego still had on me. I had returned from Nebraska and was back in San Francisco when this happened. In the Order, we were all assigned daily chores in addition to our regular jobs, studies, classes, and spiritual work. As you can tell, we didn't have much personal time except for some weekends. At the time of this experience I was the head of the kitchen detail, which meant I was responsible for cleaning up the kitchen after meals. After we were all done washing the dishes, scrubbing the floors and general clean-up, I was to inspect the area to make sure everything was completed. The head cook would then come and check to make sure we had done it properly. For whatever reason, the head cook and I just did not get along. You know the type of person that just rubs you the wrong way? We had already had a few disagreements in the short time we had known each other. After the clean-up, I was in my room studying when I heard someone on the intercom system calling my name and telling me that the head cook wanted to see me downstairs in the kitchen. I immediately knew that he was going to tell me the job had not been completed to his satisfaction. My ego immediately responded with a thought, "Who the hell does he think he is? We did the job exactly as it should have been done." I caught myself and told myself to calm down, to go listen to what he had to say and do whatever he said needed to be done, without any reaction. I knelt down for a moment and prayed for the peace to accept what the cook had to say without reacting. I walked down the stairs, reminding myself to keep calm, to see the cook as my brother and accept what he had to say. I reached the bottom of the stairs and saw the cook standing at the end of the long hallway leading to the kitchen. As I walked toward him I kept praying for peace to remain calm and not to react. When I reached him, he told me that the kitchen floor was still dirty. With immediate anger I responded, "What do you mean the floor is dirty? I checked it and it is fine. You don't know what you are talking about. I'm not about to clean it again when it has already been done right." I was livid and, of course, I acted completely opposite to the way I had intended. The ego still had my number and I knew it. This gives you a slight indication of the mountain I had to climb to reach a state of mind that would allow me to relinquish the ego. I know my prayers for calm were heard, but there were still a ton of old beliefs and anger in me that needed to be healed and released before I could begin to experience the peace I so longed for.

At this time, the focus for most souls seeking the truth should be the understanding that **what you do to others is what you are literally doing to yourself.** Understanding this law leads us into higher and higher wisdom. This is like walking a path that becomes clearer and brighter with each step that we take.

In the Order, students were brought into different initiations, depending on their level of consciousness. In my second year in the Order, Father Paul and a Master Teacher were working on my solar plexus, bringing me into the initiation of illumination. They repeatedly asked me if I could see my inner Light. It became very humorous to them as they laughed because the light they were witnessing was so vast and expansive, yet I was unaware of this because my spiritual sight had not yet been opened. It's interesting that a person can have these spiritual experiences while still dealing with their ego.

After two years in the Order, I was ordained as a priest on July 4, 1971. Unfortunately, the insecurity and anger that had plagued me most of my life was still a constant companion. Even though I was with men and women of like mind in the Order, I still could not open up and bond with others. I did a lot of teaching and counseling as a priest, but I did not feel the peace and love I knew were needed to be a true spiritual teacher.

In my third year of the Order, I had a memorable experience with a light being not of this world, while sitting on a park bench. Maybe he was sent to assist me where I was stuck. I was sitting on a park bench eating a sandwich, there were no people in the park and there was open space all around me, so I could see if anyone was nearby. I looked up from my sandwich for a moment and there was a man approaching my bench who sat down next to me. I don't recall seeing him walking over toward the bench I was sitting on. He was looking intently into my solar plexus chakra. I calmly asked him, "Are you part of the White Brotherhood?" and he replied with a very warm smile, "No, they wear white robes!" He kept focusing on my solar plexus and I intuitively knew he was working on me and assisting me in some way. He then stood up and said, "Good afternoon." I wasn't looking directly at him when he stood up and when

I did turn to see him, he was gone! There was no sign of him in any direction from the open space all around me.

Throughout my time in the Order, there were many revelations and experiences regarding my spiritual purpose and who I was. I was in the Order for about four years when suddenly, Father Paul left his body. He called me on the phone shortly before he left his body to tell me that he was "cutting all ties." I didn't understand and I thought he meant that he would be doing a lot more travel. After his death, I learned through a series of mystical visitations that Father Paul wanted me to take his place as the head of the Order. I was very honored by his request, but this was not the path that I was intended to take.

Another revelation was when I had an experience of being in the chapel for forty days and forty nights, practicing silence. I would leave the chapel to use the washroom and to eat, and other than this I remained in the chapel even to sleep. After thirty days, I was having lunch and I noticed the priests gathering and talking while looking over at me. Some Master Teachers approached and began observing me with their eyes wide. One priest walked over and sat at my table while continually observing my aura and glancing over at the other priests who were smiling. I knew they were looking at my light even though I couldn't see it.

During my ordination as a priest, Father Paul turned to the group and said, "The first one has returned." At that time, I was not cognizant of what that meant. And throughout my years as a priest, I would receive audible messages from Jeshua during critical junctures of my spiritual journey. Experiences like these were symbolic of the great blessings that lay in store for me.

I was in the Order for nine years when I had a very vivid experience in which Jeshua appeared to me and told me he was going to place me on a different path. I was in Boston then, and the thought of leaving the Order had not previously crossed my mind for quite some time. A month after this visitation, I appeared before the Order council and requested a sabbatical. After a year away from the Order I felt no inner urging to return, so I wrote to the council informing them of my resignation.

I recall one of the most beautiful messages I received in the Order from Jeshua in which he said to me, "Know that you are beloved of God and your works glorify His Creation."

I had received a lot of Grace in communing with highly spiritually evolved men and women in the Order. I experienced purification and transformation that was invaluable. Probably one of the most important tools that I learned during my time in the Order was how to still my mind and be aware that I am the observer of my thoughts and not the thinker. I will always be very grateful for the accelerated spiritual progress I experienced while I was in the Holy Order of MANS, which put me on the path of the full relinquishment of the ego.

Over the following twenty years, I would passionately explore different spiritual paths, seeking the fulfillment and culmination of my spiritual awakening. Later, I would discover *A Course in Miracles*, where I recognized this path as being the doorway to my final destination.

I stayed in Boston for a year to work and save some money. A year later, I left Boston and moved to Marin County in California. One year later I met a soul mate who would have a big impact in my life. Her name was Linda and I met her at a spiritual lecture in Marin. She intuitively recognized me immediately as I walked into the hall and approached me after the lecture. We talked after the lecture as if we had known each other for years. We were together for almost twenty-nine years before her sudden and totally unexpected departure from Earth on May 2, 2010. I will speak more about the impact that her departure had on my life later. When I met her, she was very involved and devoted to a spiritual group called Siddha Yoga and because of the connection I had with Linda, I also became very involved with Siddha Yoga for fifteen years. The leader of Siddha Yoga at the time I joined the group was Swami Muktananda. I took my first two-day intensive with Muktananda shortly after I joined the group in New York. I had a very powerful experience in this intensive when Muktananda gave me "the touch." This experience was consistent with everything I had been shown about my life path. I had many beautiful experiences with Siddha Yoga and received a great deal of grace.

At this time I was still very much in the process of unraveling the false ego that still resided in me. This process of dissolving the ego would continue for many more years before it was complete.

About a year later, I learned that a nearby Yogananda community was going to be giving a Kriya Yoga Initiation. I felt this would be a beautiful opportunity to receive Grace from a beloved Spiritual Master. I was deeply inspired by

Paramahansa Yogananda in the book, *Autobiography of a Yogi*.

Within the year of my Kriya Yoga Initiation, a friend of ours told Linda to have me read the book, *A Course in Miracles*, because she knew of my deep desire to know the Truth. I ignored this message until the third time, when I decided there must be a reason, so I purchased the book and began the course study. *A Course in Miracles* opened a whole new spiritual understanding, which led me to my destination of God Realization!

Throughout my life I was guided to various spiritual paths, which aided me in the dismantling process of my ego. Eventually, I experienced the need to release all identifications with anything or anyone being the mediator between myself and God. In the final step there is nothing between you and God, as all is One.

Reflection Five

The process of unraveling the ego is the most important and difficult task a soul will ever take on and the end result leads to spiritual realization and liberation. The dismantling of the ego will bring forth the darkest hours on our spiritual journey and can take on physical, mental, and emotional discomfort. Faith is the most important tool while walking through this process. Understanding this can help you stay on course with this enormous task. The following spiritual practice was of great benefit in my spiritual awakening: Observe your thoughts without any identification. This process requires intense focus, so it is suggested to do exercises that improve your concentration, such as focusing on a candle flame. Deeply still the mind and observe the mechanisms of the egoic mind.

Six

The Search for Truth

O ur search for truth is a journey of seeking self-understanding and the realization of who we truly are. When we have finally surrendered the illusion of our false self and the illusion of so-called physical existence, we will have realized our Oneness with God.

You speak of a Oneness with God a lot. What do you mean by that?

Let me explain this idea through an analogy. Imagine an infinitely brilliant large diamond with an infinite number of the most beautiful facets. The diamond would represent the wholeness of God, and the facets of the diamond would represent each individual soul, which God originally created. God is totally aware of each facet and each facet is totally aware of itself, God, and all other facets. There is an infinite loving exchange going on within this ever-expanding diamond. Each soul also experiences God and every other soul as themselves. I know this is a lot to take in, but I hope this gives you some idea of what Oneness means. It's not something that can be understood by the intellect; it must be experienced to a certain degree to have an understanding of what this means. We are all guaranteed that at some point on this journey, we will all become the embodiment of that which I am writing about. The more individuals who awaken on Earth, the quicker this process will unfold for all souls. We must remember that out of all the souls that were created in the beginning, only a relatively few of them have taken this journey into the illusion of Earth-existence and seeming separation from God. Many other souls are going through similar experiences on other planes. What an amazing, joyful reunion that will take place when the last soul finally awakens to Oneness.

We are currently in a time of the most miraculous transformation that this world has ever seen. The opportunities for spiritual transformation have never been so available to the masses. In this age, many souls will be able to move into the fifth dimension and beyond. In the 1960s, a singing group called The Impressions recorded a song called "People Get Ready," which is about a train that picks people up from coast to coast, but a person has to be ready to get on board. Similarly, we must do whatever we can to prepare ourselves to get aboard this spiritual train of transformation that so many are now experiencing all over the world. This spiritual transformation will carry us into a higher dimension filled with much greater light, life, and love. When Jeshua walked the earth, he stated that he had come to bring us a more abundant life (John 10:10). We now have the opportunity to partake of that abundant life, if we choose to surrender the illusion of the ego. Our true nature consists of Unconditional Love and a Peace that is beyond all understanding. Be patient with yourself as you walk this journey and you will eventually reach your goal. The joy and innocence you will eventually experience is indescribable and unfathomable.

My search for truth, in this life, began consciously when I was twenty-six. As I have shared before, this was not an easy journey for me and yet there is nothing else and no other path that I would have preferred to travel. I have now reached a state of mind in which I can say unequivocally that there is nothing even close to the joy and freedom one experiences as they begin to get some glimpses of who they truly are. As we let go of the illusion of who we thought we were, a deep sense of peace and fulfillment fills our being. This sacred realization opens the door to our Oneness with God. Each soul must make this journey on their own, although they will receive plenty of help on the way. Others can light the way and make it easier to see the obstacles on the path, but actually walking this path is the task each soul must do on their own.

A new soul on the path will be unable to understand many of the deeper truths until a multitude of their false concepts are released. Imagine a person living in a completely darkened house for years without any light whatsoever. Now, what do you think would happen if that person were to walk out of his completely darkened house into a very bright sunny day? He would be blinded by the light as his eyes would not be able to take the brilliance of the light. Instead, he would slowly have to adjust his eyes to the light. A small candle could be lit a couple of rooms from where the man is. Gradually, he would be able to walk into the room where a candle is lit without being uncomfortable. After a while, a soft lamp could be lit and so on.

I know absolutely that this world is not real, that it exists only in our mind as a dream and yet again, I want to stress that this dream is playing a very important role in the expansion of God's Creation. I know how real it seems to be because I have experienced my fair share of pain in this life and many others. As the light within one grows, so does the compassion for the suffering that mankind is enduring. Realizing who we are will bring about the end of all suffering.

If this world is not real, as you say, why does it seem so real to everyone?

It is because of the egoic belief that we are an individual, separate from all other individuals. As I have been guided to write this in order to bring Light into the darkness for all those seeking the Truth, I will continue to bring more clarity on this idea in many ways throughout this book. For now, let me tell you a story to hopefully shed some light on how this dream seemed to manifest.

Once, there lived two small boys who had the most loving parents imaginable. The father owned the most popular restaurant in all the land. People would come from all parts of the world to eat there because the food was so delicious. There was a great variety of delightful foods, whether it was for a child of three or a gourmet chef. Another unique thing about this establishment was that the food was all free. The father had more money than he could ever spend, so he saw no need to charge for the food. He just loved seeing the happy faces of the people after they had eaten a big meal. The mother was a most loving, nurturing and happy woman who loved her children more than anything. They lived in a beautiful mansion with servants who were always ready to meet any needs the children had. The children had countless playmates and they played in the vast expanse on the grounds of the mansion. The children were literally in paradise.

One summer night, as the younger son got ready for bed, something very strange happened. A very charming young man appeared to him out of nowhere and told the son that he could have his own restaurant, which would be even better than his father's. The young man claimed that people would come from all over to eat at his restaurant and that he would become very famous. The younger son loved the idea of owning his own operation and being a celebrity, so he asked his visitor how he could accomplish this. The charming man told him that he would take care of everything and to pack what he needed and leave his father's land. Without a word to his parents or brother, the son gathered many of his father's servants and left the grounds of the mansion in the middle of the night and went out on his own. He had great ambitions of building his own restaurant, where he would charge people large sums of money to eat there, unlike his father who gave it away. After many days of travel, the son finally reached the end of his father's grounds and entered into a very dry and desolate place. The son decided that this would be the place where he would build his establishment so that he could intercept people going to his father's restaurant and direct them to eat at his restaurant. His servants were told to erect a restaurant similar to his father's. When everything was completed, the son told his servants to start enticing travelers into the new establishment by whatever means necessary.

The food at the son's restaurant tasted bad in comparison to his father's and many people got sick after eating there, but he added entertainment, which distracted the customers. When people started complaining about the food, the son simply added more glitz to distract people from how they felt. He also charged exorbitant prices, but people paid the price because of the alluring entertainment. Meanwhile, the son's parents would daily send their servants to bring the boy home, but the boy refused.

After a number of years, a great drought hit the land where the son lived and there was no food to serve the customers. The son began to starve and so he began begging for food from people who were on the way to eat at his father's restaurant. They told the son that there was no need to go hungry because there was a restaurant on the grounds of the mansion where he could have all the food he wanted for free. The son got angry at the people when they told him this and yelled and cursed at them for telling him such a ridiculous lie. He had forgotten who he was.

The boy's parents were now very concerned because the boy would curse and beat the servants whom they had sent to bring him home and accused them of lying to him and wanting to take his property which, by the way, was absolutely worthless. Finally, his parents decided to send the elder son to fetch his younger brother before he died of starvation. They thought that if their lost son would see his brother, that he might come to his senses and return home. When the elder brother saw his sibling, his heart almost broke. Here was his brother, heir to a vast fortune, in rags, emaciated and starving. He also saw that the light had gone out of his younger brother's eyes and he knew that it would be difficult to communicate with him. The older brother started telling his brother about their home and how it was filled with unlimited bounty, beauty, joy, and love and that all he needed to do was return home with him and he would be welcomed with the greatest and most joyful party he could imagine. For a moment, there was even a little bit of recognition in the younger brother's eyes.

Now, wouldn't you, as the reader, think that there is really no decision for the lost son to make, here? It's a slam dunk. You go home with your brother to a land where the word "lack" does not exist. But no, after hearing his brother, the lost son decided that his sibling was also lying to him and started beating him with a stick and chased him away. When the parents heard of this, they were very sad.

The beautiful mansion and restaurant are symbolic of our true home. The dry, desolate place where the son built his own restaurant is symbolic of the physical world and a state of mind that is separated from God. The charming young man who enticed the son is symbolic of the false ego.

Now, let's close the story with a happy ending. Because of his suffering, hunger, and loneliness, the younger son finally had a heart opening and realized his great mistake and began his long journey home. After a very long and arduous journey, the son could finally see the mansion in the distance and his heart was filled with joy. Just then, the alarm clock went off and the younger son woke up and realized he had been dreaming. It had been a dreadful dream and he was so happy that none of that had actually happened. He ran to his father's and mother's bedroom and gave them a big hug. He then went to his older brother's bedroom and gave him a big hug. When the parents and brother of the younger son saw him, they recognized that there was something very different about him. His eyes were filled with light and his whole body was emanating much more light than the day before. They realized that something very dramatic had happened to him during the night.

This story contains a great truth. Our journey on the spiritual path will eventually awaken the light within us and help us to wake up from this dream.

How do we start the process of waking up?

The process begins with a conscious decision to embark on a spiritual journey, which will lead to the realization that this world is not real and that we are not this individual that most people believe we are. The process of awakening eventually leads to our letting go of illusion and to the realization of our Oneness with God. A very strong desire to know the truth is necessary to successfully embark on the spiritual journey to awakening.

Why is that?

The journey to spiritual awakening is a difficult one because it is swimming against the current of the beliefs of our world. This journey is one that the false ego wants no part of. Our will must transcend the will of the ego if we are to transcend the illusion of the world. Believe me, the ego wants no part of this journey and will do everything in its power to prevent that from happening. Actually, the ego has no power unless we continually give it the only power it has, which is our belief that we are the ego.

Imagine that you are lost in a deep, dark cave and have no idea how to get out. Many have tried to escape but were never heard from again. More than anything, you desire to find your way out of the cave. Finally, one person discovers the way out and comes back with a map that shows you how to free yourself. You must follow the map precisely in order to find your way out, otherwise you will continue to be trapped.

The map represents the truth. The truth is a great spiritual light and when it is fully accepted, illuminates our perception and allows us to see and know the difference between truth and illusion. Without light, we will continue to stumble around in the darkness of this world.

The spiritual light coming into the world at this time is so powerful that it won't take as much effort to find our way out of the darkness. The Holy Spirit, that part of our mind that is connected to God, is our key in helping us to awaken from this nightmare we are dreaming. This part of our mind knows that the world is not real but also knows that we believe it is real. Its job is to help us awaken to the knowing that we are innocent and that the seeming separation from God never actually occurred.

We don't have to try and become perfect to enter paradise. The spiritual path is a journey of great awakening. The truth is that we have never done anything wrong. Many people believe we have to be a spiritual martyr and continually offer sacrifices to God to get into Heaven. God does not desire sacrifices. **When we offer sacrifices to atone for our so-called sins, we are actually giving reality to the identity of the false self.** God only wants us to awaken to the great reality of who we truly are. On that note, I will mention something now that may shock many people: **It is not what you physically do in the world that determines your awakening. Your actions have nothing to do with it. Your awakening will take place when you realize that you are not the false ego and that in reality you are infinitely more than you could have ever imagined.**

You are not the individual you believe you are. You truly are One with God. The true transformation takes place in our hearts and minds. When this transformation takes place, the power you will awaken within you is Pure Unconditional Love. Through the presence of our Unconditional Love, many will be awakened simply by being in our presence.

Please don't think that what I am saying gives a person license to do whatever he wants. I have mentioned before that **everything that seems to be happening outside of us is really happening in our mind.** The images projected by our mind will always be in accordance with our beliefs and we will suffer the consequences, or benefits, of those beliefs. **Simply put, we are not the person we have been identifying with over countless reincarnations.** In this one statement, when fully understood, is the Divine Key into the Kingdom of Heaven. This book is all about the process of relinquishing that false self within you which has caused you so much pain and hardship for so many incarnations.

The proper state of mind is to look past the illusion of the world and begin to see the perfection in everyone we come in contact with. We must be careful not to see them as their physical condition, because then we would just be giving more validity to an illusion. We can serve our fellow man best by acknowledging their spiritual perfection. It is a challenging process to see beyond the physical appearance of things and to try to see the perfection in all things. Yet, it is extremely important to develop this spiritual perspective because **how we see the world and others is what we are creating for ourselves. Whenever we help anybody in any way, we are literally helping ourselves.**

Believe it or not, God doesn't care how good we believe we have been, or how many prayers we have said. He loves us all the same, regardless of how we believe we have lived our lives. **There is no such thing as a God that judges or punishes us.** This world that we seem to live in is a dream. Will we be punished for having a nightmare? The only thing that punishes us is our identification with the false ego.

There is one big piece to this puzzle that must also be understood: Even though in reality we have never done anything wrong, we are living in an illusionary world that operates under a universal law. That law is the law of cause and effect, often called "karma." As long as our belief system is one of separation, we will be affected by the law of karma. Whatever we do, think, and say activates that law and we meet the effects of these thoughts and actions in our daily lives. This law is one of the greatest teachers, if we are open to accepting the fact that what we experience is what we created or what we have chosen to experience. There are no victims in this world, even though many believe that they are victims. The effects we are experiencing may not have been created in this lifetime, but eventually the scales of the law of cause and effect must be balanced. These scales do not necessarily have to be balanced in a harsh, negative way. Negative karma can be offset through good deeds and service to others.

The ultimate process we have to go through regarding freeing ourselves from this illusion, is that **eventually we will need to relinquish our belief in the identity of the individual we believe we are.** I speak about this process many times here in different ways in order for it to start permeating the consciousness of the one reading this book. This process does not have to be done in this particular lifetime, as the great, great majority of mankind is not ready to take this final step into the Oneness with God. Anyone attracted to reading this book is either ready for this final step or is open to beginning this process.

We live in a hologram and everything happening in this hologram is unreal, it is a projection of our state of consciousness. As a person begins to release negativity from their mind, it makes it much easier to understand the truth of who we are. Through positive actions and thoughts, we will eventually start to get glimpses of the nature of God as this is truly who we are.

This world, our bodies and the physical universe are not real. The path back to reality requires us to go through a process of awakening to who we are not and finally realizing who we truly are. We need to open up to our inner spiritual light so that we can wake up from the dream we are having. As our inner Light becomes brighter, we will come to the realization that we are God and the Light of God will manifest on Earth through us.

I know this may sound grandiose to many, but God is One and we are all a part of that Oneness, and yet the uniqueness of who we are, the "**I AM THAT I AM**" will always be part of our eternal consciousness.

Many people have had very clear realizations of the illusion of this world. Edgar Allan Poe stated, "All that we see or seem is but a dream within a dream." Carl Jung, a great influential thinker of the twentieth century said, "Who looks outside, dreams. Who looks inside, awakens." All that we seem to be experiencing here on Earth is but a dream. It is not real. Many physicists now overwhelmingly agree that we live in a simulation, or a virtual reality universe.

Even though none of this is real, there is an extraordinary purpose for living in and experiencing this dream world. I will go into this subject in more detail in a later chapter.

Reflection Six

On your journey of seeking the truth, many obstacles will be placed in your path. You are swimming against the currents of beliefs of the world. Preparing for transformation, out of the false ego's grip of your mind, requires releasing false concepts and belief systems. Begin contemplating belief systems and concepts that are of a denser nature such as unforgiveness, resentment, jealousy, fear, and anger. Understanding and surrendering these false concepts begins to relinquish darkness, allowing more and more light, love and peace to transform you. This requires your full attention and desire.

As the Light becomes brighter within you, the Truth will be more fully and clearly revealed to you. You will begin to experience an infinite loving exchange going on within you. As your energy frequency begins to transform in your Heart and Mind, you will become less and less comfortable with false beliefs. You will experience a deep sense of peace while growing in compassion, leading to your full liberation. The spiritual journey requires us to go through a process of awakening to who we are not and realizing who we truly are. This eventually leads to the realization that we are God and the great Light and Grace of God will manifest through us.

Seven

The Obstacle of Pride

Throughout my entire spiritual journey and practices, there was a very big block that escaped my spiritual vision. It was such a part of my character that I could not see it. It was like having an elephant in my living room and not being able to see it and yet anyone really close to me could. You might wonder why someone so dedicated to his spiritual path could possibly be so blind to this one big aspect of himself. Interestingly, this character flaw was actually the initial cause of the soul slowly losing its connection with God in the beginning of time. It was the cause of our fall from innocence.

You've probably heard of the story in which the Archangel Lucifer was cast out of Heaven. Lucifer was referred to as the Morning Star, the brightest star of all in the angelic realm. This story implies that because Lucifer became so enamored with himself, he actually felt that he could usurp God's throne and take control of Heaven. Of course, this was impossible since God is infinite and All That Is. Lucifer's false pride was the beginning of a huge downfall, which eventually brought us to where we are now. There's the old saying, **"Pride goeth before a fall."**

We seem to be entrapped in human bodies we believe are us and we identify with everything that happens to these bodies. We typically never even question who we truly are until we finally reach a place of such desperation that we either bemoan our fate or we begin the search for the truth and what life is all about.

I had advanced so far on the path but was sort of stuck at one point because of this huge barrier that stood before me that I could not see for a very long time. My partner at the time, was the first one who really tried to get me to see my pride. Even after telling me many times, I simply discarded it as her seeing something that was not there. My current partner finally got this truth through to me after also having tried many times. Finally, as I was going through a very humbling experience in my life, I was open enough to hearing what my partner had been saying and could finally see this major fault in myself. This acknowledgment of my false pride finally opened the door for healing and going through my initiation of entering into full Union with God.

My wife and I had gone to Mexico where we had purchased a timeshare at this beautiful resort right on the coast. I got involved in a scam that started about a year after I purchased the timeshare.

I received a phone call from a solicitor stating that a businessman was interested in purchasing as many of the timeshares from the resort in which my wife and I owned.

They said he wanted to send his employees there for vacation. As scams go, this was a very thorough and thought-out process of deception that ensued over several months.

My wife could hear the conversation from my speakerphone and was motioning to me that it was a scam. She explained that the call sounded overseas and she could feel it was a scam and asked me to drop the whole thing.

I continued to accept calls from this outfit and even agreed to sell our timeshare to them. Over many conversations and make-believe lawyers, make-believe holding fee laws in which I made three separate bank wires, I had lost sight of reason.

Over the course of three months, my wife would ask me from time to time if I had disconnected all ties. The first time she asked, I told her that I had not.

She literally got on her knees pleading with me to stop all contact with them because she knew it was a scam.

I disregarded her pleas and rolled my eyes, feeling frustrated with her "overreaction." Months passed as I continued to wire them money. By this time our bank began to recognize a scam and they instantly closed my bank account! When this happened I was so startled it was like I came out of a trance. It was as if I was finally awakened from a very bad dream I was having in which

I had surrendered and lost a great amount of money. I realized that my pride had prevented me from accepting the insight my wife was trying to offer me. We both knew that she was better at sniffing these sorts of things out than I, yet I refused to work with her on this and I trusted a complete stranger. My Pride also opened a door to a certain amount of negative energies influencing and distracting me from my spiritual focus.

So, this was my Huge Lesson!

My wife was in a spiritual retreat in Colorado at the time and she called me to say she wished I had joined her and I replied, "That's alright because the retreat has come to me! I am learning a valuable lesson that is revealing my ego in a very clear way that I could never see before! This is what my late wife kept saying to me and what you have been trying to get across to me and I can see it all so clearly now!" I remember saying, "This valuable lesson about my pride was worth the money I lost." Within two weeks I had completely forgiven the main front man, deemed "Michael." I quickly looked at all of this with such humor, like characters in a play. What's even more ironic and even more comical about what happened was that I had worked for the U.S. Department of the Treasury as a financial analyst for fifteen years! My wife was very moved by how quickly I was able to transcend the dynamics into a neutral event.

She also had to go through a big lesson in forgiving me for not heeding her warnings. This was a spiritual process for each of us. As we know, on our spiritual journeys we are always presented with deep challenges and opportunities for spiritual growth.

I accepted this as part of my karma and part of my lessons that my own higher self was bringing forth for my greater spiritual awakening.

The Merriam-Webster dictionary defines pride as, "The quality of having an excessively high opinion of oneself or one's importance." False pride is the ego consciousness ruling our thoughts. Whereas pure Pride is the realization of who we truly are in God. False pride may not be a sin, but it is a huge barrier to spiritual insight and becoming who we truly are. The only place these things exist is in the belief system in our minds. I do emphasize that false pride can come in many guises, so spiritual aspirants, beware.

How do we free ourselves from these binding concepts?

We free ourselves by letting go of the false belief that we are this individual personality we are so identified with. This identification creates all the suffering and separation that we seem to experience. This is why Jeshua stated that a person must give up their life to find life (Matthew 16:24-26).

Let me share another story with you that will hopefully shed further light on this subject. Once there was a planet in which all the people in that world walked around for twenty-four hours a day with a huge bag full of heavy rocks. One day, a being from a very spiritually advanced plane visited this strange world. The visitor, let's call her Mary, was very curious as to why these people were punishing themselves by carrying heavy bags, which completely restricted their movement. Mary decided to talk to one of them to find out why they were doing this to themselves. Mary could see very clearly that all these people needed to do was loosen the straps of their bags and free themselves. Mary flew down to talk to a man who had a bag much heavier than most and asked him why he just didn't take the bag off so he could move with total freedom. The man started telling Mary all about his life and all the misfortunes he had experienced. Mary listened with interest and when the man was finally finished telling her about his woeful life she said, "I understand what you are saying, but I still don't understand why you carry this heavy bag with you. Why don't you just take it off?" The man had no idea what Mary was talking about and off he went carrying his heavy weight.

The man carrying the weight is synonymous with just about everybody on planet Earth. Anyone who is not free of their limiting beliefs and false identifications, which restrict their movement and enjoyment of life, are like the people carrying the heavy bags.

Jeshua said, "Be it unto you as you believe" (Matthew 8:13). **It is only our identification with and our attachment to the false self, which we believe we are, that binds us to the karma of our particular mind and body.** Can you accept the realization that you are not the individual you think you are? Are you willing to mentally and emotionally die to everything you have ever believed about yourself and about the world in order to find out who you really are? You are definitely not who you think you are. The greatest of all truths is that you are truly God walking on Earth because God is all that ever was, is, and ever will be. The great, great majority of Earth's population would take that last statement as blasphemy, being totally unacceptable to the egoic mind. The false ego will never accept this truth because when a soul fully accepts this truth, the false ego will disappear into the nothingness from whence it *seemed* to arise.

Karma plays a part in making it more difficult to see this truth. Just as you need light to see in a completely darkened room, you need spiritual light to truly understand what I am saying. Heavy karma makes the seeing of this truth much more difficult. For those of us who have consciously or unconsciously identified with guilt to the degree that it has become such a part of who we think we are, it really takes a great deal of light to see it and even more light to stop identifying with it. This is what happened to me regarding pride. It was such a part of me that even with the spiritual light I was carrying, it took a very humbling experience to finally allow me to be open to seeing it clearly. The Grace of God, forgiveness, healing of karma and the removal of conscious and unconscious influences can assist us in shifting from a state of unconsciousness to consciousness, from unawareness to awareness. This is how I found peace with this prideful experience I mentioned above.

How would you suggest releasing the bags we are carrying?

In order to experience who we truly are, we must be willing to totally let go of the false ego, which is the identification and attachment to the belief in who we think we are. We need to be willing to let go of our relationship to all our belief systems. This includes the belief in everything we have ever known about this world. This truly is the willingness to go through the crucifixion of the false ego and renounce all belief in the individual we believed we were. When you fully awaken, you will not lose contact with the people close to you but you will see them in a totally different Light. Your Divine Transformation will also be a great light to those close to you so they will also be able to see more clearly, if they are seeking the truth.

A very powerful practice is to make this declaration with every ounce of your being as often as you can: **"I renounce all belief in this individual that I have** identified with all my life. I renounce all belief in this world of illusion that I thought was real." Do this constantly and it will start to have powerful effects in your life. Along with this, rather than identifying with everything that happens to you, be the impersonal observer of all that happens to this individual, without any attachment to what is taking place or to what the experience seems to be. It is like watching a twenty-four-hour-a-day movie in which the star of the movie, the false you, goes through many different experiences. By being the impersonal observer, you begin to detach from the body/mind that you thought was you. Be the observer and not the victim.

Regarding pride, I highly encourage any spiritual aspirant to truly search very deeply within themselves to locate any false pride and to do everything within their power to release this biggest-of-all stumbling blocks. You will probably need assistance from someone who is spiritually advanced in order to assist you in this process.

I send you all my love and blessings in this holy endeavor.

Reflection Seven

Pride can be very difficult to unveil because it is so ingrained in a person's personality. A person needs to be very aware of all aspects of their personality in order to uncover the pride within themselves. Other aspects of pride are superiority, self-centeredness, self-importance, judgment, the unwillingness to forgive, and vainness, to name a few. Discovering these denial aspects in ourselves can be very powerful. We free ourselves by letting go of the false belief that we are this individual personality that we are so identified with. It is our identification with and our attachment to who we believe we are that binds us. This is the pride of an illusionary ego that does not, nor ever has, existed; it's not real. Explore that you are not the individual that you think you are. Become willing to mentally and emotionally die to everything you have ever believed about yourself and about the world in order to find out who you truly are. Become the observer of all that happens to this individual without any attachment to what is taking place or to what the experience seems to be. Begin to detach from the body/mind that you thought was you. Become the observer and not the victim.

Eight

Free Will or Destiny?

The question of whether our experiences here on Earth are predestined or a result of our choices is a philosophical question that has been pondered throughout history.

Free Will is the most powerful tool we have toward finding the Truth of who we are. However, many astrologers say that a person with many planets with fixed signs in their chart have less of a choice as to what their path may be. These fixed aspects may be in the chart of a soul who has created a lot of karma and now needs to start paying off some of that debt. He therefore has, by karmic necessity, taken on a more restricted path in that life. Fixed aspects in the chart of a highly evolved soul are for the intention of fulfilling a particular purpose the soul chose to take on in that lifetime. Yet in both cases, there is the element of Free Will, which can always change the direction of their life. **A person experiencing a more restricted life, because of karma, would have less use of his Free Will; but as long as we are in the world of duality and have Free Will, anything is possible.**

Is it possible for someone with a lot of karma to fully awaken?

Yes, it is possible, if the soul with that karma *could somehow* extract himself from his identification and attachment with the illusions the false ego presents. This is the path less traveled and requires tremendous focus and discipline. It would be like giving a book to a person in a darkened room with no lights and asking them to read it. A person needs the spiritual light to see where she is going and to make choices that are in accordance with the relinquishing of the ego. The reason it would be possible is that in reality, the soul has never done anything wrong. So how hard can it be to release something that does not exist? The main obstacle to this release is that in the darkness, the ego is in control and it will do everything it can to continue to keep the soul in the darkness. The ego, even though it doesn't really exist, has a self-preservation instinct.

I came into this life with the intention of taking on the fullness of the Christ Consciousness and fulfilling whatever spiritual purpose it was that God sent me here to do. I have wondered at times whether I could have stepped off my spiritual path and gone on a different and darker journey because of the difficulties I faced in life. I really can't say. I have known some very spiritually evolved beings who held a lot of light but had not fully relinquished their ego and thus made choices that led them down some dark paths.

There are also very highly evolved souls that chose to take on very difficult experiences in life in order to take on some of the karma of the world. In this realm of duality, it is even possible for these highly evolved souls to lose their way because of the difficult path they chose. Think of the amazing love and courage these souls have for humanity to take on such a difficult mission that could even possibly go astray.

In one of his trance sessions, Edgar Cayce said, **"A man's will creates his destiny."** This is more along the lines of how free will or destiny operates. I mentioned earlier that in my experiences in the Holy Order of MANS, there was such a strong egoic pull to leave the Order in that first year, that it took every ounce of my will to stay the course. Was it predestined that I should stay, or was it free will? **There are some predestined experiences in each of our lives because of karma and choice, but it is the free will of an individual that determines whether these experiences become something greater or lesser.**

Many souls come onto Earth under extremely difficult circumstances because of past karma, but even these difficulties can be transcended through the use of the will. There is a saying, "Know that at any time, free will can draw the sword out of the stone." That is how powerful our will is. It comes down to how much we want something and how far we are willing to apply ourselves to get it. How strongly do we desire to transcend this illusion, the pain it brings and our identification with the ego? That is the question each individual will eventually have to ask themselves. There is no time limit as to when this must be done.

For those of you who are familiar with the tarot deck, there is a card entitled, "Wheel of Fortune," which represents the cycles of birth, death, and rebirth in this dream world. Some lifetimes will be easier than others, but we will continue to ride the wheel of fortune with all its ups and downs until we make a decision to wake up and get off the karmic cycle. **As long as we believe that the individual we seem to be is our true identity and that we are separate from God, our lives are, in a sense, predestined.** We will continue to ride the rollercoaster of life, with all its ups and downs, until we decide that we have had enough. **The greatest tool that we have at our disposal to awaken spiritually is our freedom of choice. The power of our free will can not only change our present conditions, but our past and future as well. Our destiny is in our hands.**

As our understanding of truth grows, we will also realize the futility of blaming someone else for anything that happens in our lives. We will know that the "outer" events taking place are all really taking place in our mind and that everything in our mind is our creation and our responsibility. If we continue to allow the ego to choose our path in life, we will continue on the karmic cycle of birth and death, with the fear of death being paramount in our minds.

A person who is enlightened will also leave the body behind, but her experience of death will be incredibly beautiful. Leaving her body at death will be like stepping out of a car that has served its purpose.

A God-Realized person will have broken the cycle of birth and death and will no longer need to reincarnate in this world, although she may decide to incarnate again to help humanity. She will not experience fear when she does leave her body, because she knows that there is no such thing as death. In fact, her experience will be one of joy. Unfortunately, most people experience death with fear, dread, and usually a lot of pain.

As we begin taking control of our destiny through our spiritual striving, the difficult astrological influences of which we were born with can be transcended.

We are the creators of our destiny, not the planets. We are also creators of the stars, not their servants.

In order to understand how free will and destiny both have their place in this illusionary world, I will explain something. When the separation from God first occurred in the mind of the souls who sought to separate themselves from God, it created a great deal of guilt and fear. These negative emotions set the stage for the creation of the false ego. The ego promised us a way out of our feelings of guilt and a new and better life. We accepted the ego's will and direction without questioning the ego's insane logic. The ego's insane logic, based on fear, will continue to create our destiny until we have made the choice to wake up. The ego's desire for everyone in this world is for us to remain asleep so it can maintain control. The masses of people are like robots, or hypnotized subjects, blindly following the insane plan of the ego. I will share more on this idea in greater detail later in this chapter.

We have within us the power to choose truth over illusion. We can choose to follow the path of awakening with the Holy Spirit as our guide. In the beginning of the spiritual path, we simply need to have a willingness to find out what Truth is. As we grow spiritually through our choices and efforts, our life and path will change accordingly. A person who makes this new choice is now moving away from the insane script of the ego onto a path which leads to that Perfect Peace that surpasses all understanding.

I had a beautiful, potent experience of this Perfect Peace. I was walking down the hall in our house when suddenly this Divine field of energy engulfed me. I sat down on the couch to fully experience this state of Perfect Peace. It is not something I can describe in words as this "state" was set apart from the constant peace I already walk with daily. This experience seemed to last about five to ten minutes, but I can't say because time does not exist in that state. It was otherworldly and cannot be described in words. **This Perfect Peace, in truth, is our natural state.**

Afterward, as I contemplated this amazing experience, I wondered if I lived in this state continually, if I would be moved to do any work of any kind, as this experience totally fulfilled any need or desire for anything else.

How can we choose the Holy Spirit as our guide, instead of the ego?

Remember, the Holy Spirit is the part of our mind we share with God. When you wake up in the morning, have the intention that you will allow the Holy Spirit to make all decisions for you during that day. Anytime you have a decision to make, silently ask the Holy Spirit to guide you in making the correct choice. Anytime you are in a situation in which you feel any type of upset, offer the situation to the Holy Spirit so that a so-called negative situation can be turned into a positive one. Make it a habit to bring the Holy Spirit into all your affairs. As you do this, you will find your life becoming much brighter and more peaceful. You are silently turning your life over to a force that is incapable of error. You are turning your life over to the Will of God. I invite you to make this your determination and declaration, as only you have the power to do this for yourself.

There is one thing I am happy to report that is absolutely predestined for each and every one of us: We will all eventually regain our full awareness of our Unity with God. There is nothing we can do that will change that outcome, although we can choose to remain asleep and continue in a state of illusion, pain, and separation for as long as we desire. God has placed no time limit as to when we choose to awaken.

"Karma" is a word that has become very popular in the last fifty years. Scientifically, the word can be described as the law of cause and effect: for every action there is an equal and opposite reaction. It is said, "What a man sows, so shall he reap" (Galatians 6:7), which is another way to describe the law of karma. **This law of karma could be called, "The universal balance scale that always keeps the author and his creation in perfect balance."** The conditions of our lives, work, finances, and our mental and emotional states are all a result of how we have used this law in the past. We activate the law of cause and effect through our beliefs, desires, and most importantly, our will. Our life experiences are simply a manifestation of our beliefs, desires, and choices through the law of cause and effect. The law of cause and effect does not take into consideration the person who is using it. This law simply produces the effects of what we think, do, and believe.

Was our destiny determined at the time we were created by God?

No, our karmic path began after we seemed to separate from God and allowed the ego to take over our lives. It was then that we started using our free will to determine our destiny. God knew when He created us that by giving us free will anything was possible, even the impossible. That is how powerful we are as extensions of God. We are literally an extension of God with all the attributes, creativeness, and power of God. At a certain point in creation, our individual soul was birthed by God using the essence of God Himself to create us.

As spiritual children, we were One with God and His creation, creating and extending God's creation as co-creators. As spiritual adolescents, some of us fell asleep and seemed to go our own way. Because of our having fallen asleep, we have forgotten our Unity with God. In spiritual maturity, we return to the state of Unity with God, referred to as "the return of the prodigal son." We return to God with much greater wisdom and light than when we left because of our seeming experiences in the seeming separation from God. When a soul finally moves into the state of Union with God, all of creation rejoices over the return of the prodigal son (Luke 15:11-32).

If we have separated from the consciousness of God, from All That Is, these are the different levels of sleep. When we fell asleep, we actually believed that the separation from God was real. Now remember, we were created in the image of God and our thoughts have unlimited powers. This belief in the separation from God created a conundrum. Separation could not possibly happen in God where all is One. There was only one place this idea could manifest and that was in a realm of unreality, as in a very deep sleep. When we dream at night, we enter a realm of the mind called the subconscious. The term "subconscious" means, "below the threshold of consciousness," in other words, unconsciousness. This illusionary dream world here on Earth is a realm of unreality, so seemingly real that the great majority of people are asleep and unaware of what is real. They believe that this dream world is their reality. The spiritual path is a process of awakening from this dream.

As we fell into a deep sleep, we created an imaginary world of illusion, which in reality does not exist. We gradually lost memory of who we were and of our connection to God. In this illusionary world, the belief in the ideas of separation, individuality, good and evil, and suffering came into being. This is the symbolism of Adam and Eve eating of the tree of the knowledge of good and evil and being cast out of the Garden of Eden. **A spiritual aspirant's task is to use his free will to awaken from this dream and remember who he truly is.**

Even in this confused world, our judicial system has compassionate laws that protect insane people from punishment for crimes they committed without their full mental faculties. If this illusionary world knows enough to have compassion for others who are not in their right minds, why do we insist on condemning ourselves for a bad dream we are having, which in reality never happened? God in no way has, or ever could, judge us. It is impossible for Love to judge. We are in a dream world, which does have a law that governs all events in that world, which is the law of cause and effect.

This world believes in time and a linear progression of events. We are repeatedly living the memories of this instant over and over in our minds. We cling to this illusion as our reality and seem to suffer, die and be born again. By clinging to our false beliefs, we sentence ourselves to continued cycles of births and deaths in a place that doesn't exist. When we are finally tired enough of all this pain, we seek a way out. Except for those who have awakened, there is no real joy in this world. There are fleeting distractions from our desperate states, but no real lasting joy. Through our free will we can change our destiny from one of desperation into one of Perfect Peace.

You keep stating that this world is a dream and never happened. I find that hard to believe.

This is the reason that most people don't even contemplate awakening because to them, this illusion is reality. Usually, it takes some traumatic event in a person's life that causes them to question what life is all about. Others experience a spiritual awakening naturally, which sets them on a path of self-discovery.

I now want to ask you a series of questions. Should we condemn a child for having a bad dream? Should the child be forced to feel guilty for a dream over which he had no control? Should children fear their parents because of a bad dream? Should children be forced to spend time in a place called purgatory—or even worse, Hell—because of a silly dream? Actually, our fears and guilt have created places like purgatory and Hell, but it was we who have condemned ourselves to these places, not some judgmental God. The great spiritual teachers of the past and present told us that we must wake up from this dream; that we must change our way of thinking and realize that, in reality, we are children of the Most High. Buddha taught that everything in this world is temporary and subject to decay and therefore could not be real (the Sūtra on Impermanence). Jeshua said that we shall know the truth and the truth will set us free (John 8:31-32). We cannot be forced to accept truth, just as a horse can be led to water but not forced to drink. It is just a matter of whether we are tired enough of being afraid of so many things that seem to be out of our control, that we start looking for something with greater meaning and a lasting reward.

When a soul comes to the full realization that this life is just a dream, it doesn't mean she has the license to do whatever she wants and be able to get away with it. We still have to abide by the universal law of cause and effect, and what we create we must experience. The realization that this world is all a dream also does not mean we have overcome the world. **We become free by the full realization that we are not the person we have identified with in the world and by accepting our Oneness with God.** We can also help ourselves to liberation by seeing the perfection in every person and situation we encounter throughout the day. We are then taking a big step toward finally seeing reality instead of illusion. This is a process that will take some time. Our willingness and vigilance to completely reverse our belief system will help immeasurably in shortening the amount of time it will take us to wake up. Each soul has free will and it is through our will that we determine our direction and experiences in life.

Imagine that you were sentenced to prison for twenty years and the judge told you that your sentence would be reduced by one year for every forty hours of hard labor you performed in the prison. I don't think there are too many of us who wouldn't put in at least forty or more hours a week in order to get out of prison as soon as possible. The problem that most of us have is that we don't realize we are in a prison. We are so asleep that we believe the life we seem to be living is the way it is supposed to be. Sincere seekers who know that this is not the life they were intended to live will do everything in their power to choose to awaken each and every moment of every day.

Buddha taught that it is imperative to seek true understanding, because only then can we begin the process of releasing the shackles of illusion that bind us. **Truth is realized by a mind willing to let go of its old beliefs and ways of doing things, in order to make room for a much greater Light.** We must come to the realization that we have been tricked by the ego into believing a complete lie. We simply need to be sincere in our desire to know the truth, which will lead us to spiritual awakening. Knowing the truth will open the way for us to forgive ourselves and the whole world for things that seemed to have happened in a dream.

I've talked to many people who seem to think the world is getting worse and not better. Outwardly, this may appear to be so. The spiritual awakening that I am referring to consists of the greater spiritual awareness, which is being realized by many individuals who are having profound effects on the consciousness of this world. We are all connected and what one thinks affects the minds of all people because of our shared consciousness.

Powerful spiritual thoughts have tremendous influence on the mind of this world. Most of us have no idea of the power of our thoughts. The printing of many spiritually inspired books has made this truth available to all mankind. A sincere seeker needs only to use their free will and apply the principles in these books to begin their awakening process. In this day and age, more and more people are ready to discover the truth.

There will also be those who are so identified with the ego that the truth is a threat to their illusionary existence. The ego knows that truth will dispel all illusion and thus end its illusionary existence, so of course it wants no part of truth. There is no judgment if a soul chooses to remain asleep, but why would a person choose to experience emptiness when Pure Unconditional Love is within us? We and we alone are the judge and jury of our own lives. As long as we continue to identify with the false ego, we will be caught up in the painful cycle of death and rebirth.

The following short story can allow us to look at the world's situation in another way:

A large ship sailing from a very wealthy country was captured by the military of a small dictatorial country. The thousands of people aboard the ship were put in prison. Years passed and the captives endured a daily life of pain, drudgery, and hopelessness. Many prisoners became so accustomed to prison life that they actually believed they were content. When word about the hijack and kidnapping finally reached the king of the wealthy nation, he sent his best troops to infiltrate the country that was ruled by a dictator. These troops landed in the dead of night and by the next morning had taken on the dress and manners of the foreigners in order to blend in and not be detected. Slowly, these special troops began to infiltrate positions of power in the dictatorial country and eventually, one was appointed as the warden of the prison. The new warden appointed many of the other special troops as guards. When all positions of importance in the prison were under the authority of the special troops, word was passed to all the prisoners that several ships from their country were on the way to rescue them.

Amazingly, some of the prisoners had completely forgotten about their homeland and paid no attention to those who had come to rescue them. Others listened at first, but then became so caught up in their routine that the message was soon forgotten. But many were overjoyed at the news and started preparing for their escape. No one knew when the ships would arrive, not even the warden. About a day before the rescue was to take place, the warden received word through a special transmission. He sent the guards into the prison to tell the inmates to get ready to leave as soon as he gave the word. Some of the inmates who had forgotten their homeland and were content to be in the prison threatened to tell the dictator about this plan, but since they could not get out of the prison grounds, it was an empty threat. The following morning at sunrise, the ships arrived and all the inmates willing to go back to their country were loaded aboard. The warden and the guards tried to talk some sense into the remaining inmates, telling them about the beauty and the joy of their home country, but the unconscious inmates would not listen and continued to threaten to tell the dictator. Finally, the warden and the guards realized it was too late and sadly had to leave their remaining countrymen in this dark prison because of their inability to remember.

It was our free will that seemingly created this illusion that caused us to fall into a deep sleep, in which we believed we had separated ourselves from God. It is this same freedom of choice that will allow us to once again awaken to our Holy Union with God.

There are so many versions of truth out there. How are we to know what the truth really is?

Truth is understood on many different levels according to a person's spiritual development. We constantly have the freedom to choose between truth and illusion. I will now appear to contradict myself by saying that **in reality there is no such thing as a will that is separate from God's Will.** The key word here is "reality." **When we reach a certain state of spiritual development, we will come to the realization that there is truly only one Will and that is the Will of God.** We are a part of God and like God, our true nature is Pure Unconditional Love and holy and divine innocence. Our true will is absolutely the same as the Will of God because we are One with God. Nothing can exist outside of God. **All that ever was and ever will be is all one thing and that is God.** When we come into full awakening and realization, we will know that **we are God in union with all that ever was and ever will be.** This is an amazing truth that should be contemplated often. **This Truth will be realized when we surrender this dream and our false identification with an ego that never existed.**

You keep saying that what I am experiencing is not really taking place, yet I can feel the pain and I know it is real.

It does seem to be very real until we begin to awaken. Our minds seem to be split. One part of our mind, which is controlled by the false ego, causes us to fully believe in the illusion and drama of this world. The other part of our mind, which is our true self, is patiently waiting until we start calling upon it for help. Once we have made the decision to wake up, the true part of our mind will begin to slowly dissolve the egoic mind, just as the sun dissipates the darkness when it begins to rise at dawn. Is it Free Will or Destiny that brings about our awakening? Both have tremendous implications in our lives but **free will triumphs over destiny in the sense that through the focused use of our will, we can change our destiny.** The question is: are we going to choose to use the unlimited power of our will to change our destiny?

Reflection Eight

Without free will, we would have no consciousness of choice. We've been given the most powerful and sacred gift, which we must use as much as possible, to separate illusion from reality. Do a retrospection to determine how you have been using your free will. Contemplate and ask yourself how you are using this gift. Free will is what makes you who you are. Are you satisfied with who you are? If not, you have the free will to change it.

We have within us the power to choose truth over illusion. The Holy Spirit is the part of our mind we share with God. Have the intention that you will allow the Holy Spirit to make all decisions for you each day. A person who makes this new choice is now moving away from the false script of the ego into a sense of Peace that surpasses all understanding.

The law of cause and effect simply produces the effects of what we think, do, and believe. Through our free will we can change our destiny from one of desperation into one of Perfect Peace. This truth is realized by a mind willing to let go of its old beliefs and ways of doing things in order to make room for a much greater light. The ego knows that truth will dispel all illusion and thus end its illusionary existence.

Nine

Prayer

Throughout my spiritual journey, there was one prayer that was always on the tip of my tongue. The prayer I am referring to is: **"Be it unto me according to Your Will Mother/Father God."** It was a light for me in my darkest hours and a healing balm when my soul was enduring many challenges. It was the staff I needed to lean on when ascending some of the rougher peaks of the spiritual mountain. It was a lighthouse when I encountered stormy seas. This prayer has been a sacred mantra for me.

As I mentioned before, my first year in the Holy Order of MANS was immensely difficult. I wanted to leave the Order so often because of the mental, emotional, and physical discomfort I experienced. Each time I had this intense desire to leave, I would go to the chapel and pray that God's Will and not my own be done. This prayer and my willingness to do God's Will were the powerful forces that allowed me to go through this process of transformation.

This particular prayer may not resonate with the way many of you pray and that is perfectly fine. Just find your own way of seeking God's Will in your life. We are all unique and have our own way of communicating with our Creator. **When we experience a sacred state in which we consciously commune with God, our spirit will flow through us and the perfect words will naturally come out of our mouth without any thought.** When his disciples asked Jeshua how to pray, he gave them the Lord's prayer. In this prayer he stated, "Thy Will be done on Earth as it is in Heaven" (Matthew 6:9-13). Just talk from your heart when you pray to God and you will be heard.

In our prayers, we can surrender all our worries and problems and accept that our mind be healed, which can bring us great comfort. Praying is an intimate way of communing with our true Nature, which is God. When we begin to make that intimate connection with God in prayer, our own higher self will do the talking and you will feel the bliss of that sacred communion. The important thing in prayer is our willingness to surrender our individual will to the One Will that governs all that is. We are One with God and so God's Will, in truth, is our will. In surrendering to God's Will, we are surrendering to the truth of who we are. As I began to let go of my personal will, my prayers became much more powerful. I felt a strong connection to God each time I would raise my consciousness toward Her in prayer. It was such a beautiful and blissful feeling that tears would start pouring down my face. I now understand how some saints would levitate during prayer because of the strong connection with God.

True prayer comes from the sincerity and devotion in the heart of the one saying the prayer. It is very difficult to have a deep connection with God in prayer if we perceive Him as someone who is so far beyond our reach, so far above us. We need to speak to God in a personal way as a child would speak to her mother whom she knows loves her unconditionally. **In reality, we are truly praying to our own Divine Nature.** If we are truly sincere in our prayer and speak from the heart, our prayer will be heard. That answer may come in the form of an inner voice or through something someone else says to us. The answer may also come in the form of a situation that appears in our life. God will be personal to us if we are personal to Him. We can tell Her our deepest yearnings and concerns as a child would to her mother or a trusted and loving friend. A personal relationship with God allows us to fully open our hearts in prayer. God dwells within the heart of every individual, so we cannot have a much closer, personal, and intimate relationship with anyone else other than God.

Our personal communication with God is extremely beautiful, but there is another type of prayer. This type of prayer is reflected in the way we live our lives. How do we treat others, regardless of their status in this world? How do we respond to the good fortunes and difficulties we encounter in life? A living prayer is a constant prayer without ceasing. If we live our lives in the best and highest way we know how, then we become a living prayer. I think the simplest and best way to depict a living prayer is through a story that came to me that is filled with symbolism of the journey that all lightworkers have chosen to take...

Once upon a time, very high up in the mountains, there was a beautiful kingdom where the people lived a very loving and joyous life. The king was very loving and kind and treated all his subjects as though each one was his own son or daughter. There came a point when certain citizens decided to venture out of the kingdom and descend the mountain and explore the valley below. After a number of years, the king became worried about his countrymen who had left the kingdom and were not heard from. The king called his wisest spiritual advisor and asked him to go into meditation and see how those who had left were doing.

After an hour, the spiritual advisor returned to the king and told him that his subjects who had descended the mountain were lost in the deep darkness that pervaded the whole valley. He told the king that in his meditation he was shown a brilliant diamond that emitted great light, which would help the subjects who were lost in darkness. The barrier was that the diamond was in a deep cave in the depth of a huge mountain. He told the king that the diamond was being guarded by a fierce dragon in the cave and that in order to retrieve it, someone would have to kill the dragon. He warned the king that there would be grave dangers to anyone who would enter the valley because they would also be subject to the heavy darkness that was present.

After much deliberation, the king decided that he would call upon his bravest soldiers to find out if they were willing to go into the valley to find the diamond and save their countrymen. He knew he was asking them to do something that could very well cost them their lives. The king called together his twelve most courageous and devoted warriors and asked if they would volunteer to go into the valley and find the diamond and lead their brothers and sisters back to the kingdom. He warned them about the immense dangers in the valley and that because of the darkness down there, there was a strong probability that they would temporarily forget who they were and even forget their purpose for going into the valley. He told them the light in their own hearts would always be a guiding voice to lead them home and to pay close attention to that voice. The king shared that the journey he was sending them on would be very difficult but that he knew they would succeed. The twelve warriors loved the king with all their hearts and agreed to take on this mission. After a huge celebration, they were sent off by the king and the subjects of the kingdom with deep gratitude and love.

Once the warriors reached the depth of the valley, the darkness started to take its toll. They all began to forget who they were and why they were in this strange place, but they continued on together even though they did not know where they were going.

The first people the warriors encountered were from a small village. The villagers invited the warriors to dine with them. The warriors were very hungry and the food was so delicious that one of them decided to stay and live with the villagers and learn all he could about cooking.

So, the eleven continued on with their journey and the next village they came upon was inhabited by the most beautiful women they could imagine. One of the warriors was so enticed by the beauty of the women that he decided to live in that village. Now there were only ten warriors left and they continued their journey, not really knowing where they were going or for what reason.

The next people they encountered were fierce fighters, and again one of the warriors chose to stay and learn the skills of war.

Later on, they came to another settlement where the inhabitants were experts in black magic. Once again, one of the warriors chose to stay and learn this art.

Over time, the warriors came across other villages that enticed some of them to stay. Over the next year, the group of warriors became smaller and smaller as one by one they became enamored with different facets of life in the valley. Finally, there was only one warrior left and his name was Christopher. Christopher was the bravest of all the warriors and because of his dedication, the voice within his heart began to speak to him. He slowly started to remember more and more about his purpose for coming into the valley. At that point of his journey, Christopher started encountering more and more people who directed him and told him about a large, one-hundred-foot-tall dragon who lived in a cave. They also told him about the huge diamond the dragon was protecting.

As Christopher continued his journey, he actually began to hear the loud roar of the dragon in the distance. At that point, he no longer encountered anyone as they were all too afraid to get close to where the dragon lived. He had to travel the last part of the journey alone.

As Christopher traveled on, the roar of the dragon became louder and louder so that even Christopher began to experience fear. Even through all the fear he was experiencing, the voice of guidance within him became louder and clearer and told him to be courageous and no harm would come to him. This voice gave Christopher the courage to go on, but he still had no idea how one man could possibly kill a dragon of that size. Christopher was fully committed to getting the diamond for his king and the people of the kingdom.

Then, one morning as Christopher walked over a little hill, he saw the large, dark cave where the dragon lived. Great fear filled his heart as the roar of the dragon was almost deafening. The voice within him told him to keep moving past any fear that might arise. The only thing that kept Christopher going was his desire to fulfill his king's request. With his sword in hand, Christopher entered the dark cave. He had never experienced fear in the kingdom but now it was so encompassing that he found it hard to walk, and yet he found the courage to continue moving forward. He could now sense the heat from the dragon's breath. Christopher knew that around the next corner he would face his greatest fear and challenge. His great heart was beating so fast that he had difficulty breathing. His courage was now being tested to the fullest.

Knowing that there would be a good chance that he was going to be killed by the dragon, Christopher courageously stepped around the corner to face it. To his utter amazement, there was no dragon or diamond. Then, in a flash of illumination, Christopher realized that because of his willingness to face his greatest fear for the sake of others, he had become the brilliant light that he was seeking. Through his dedication and willingness to die to fulfill the king's edict, he was transformed into the very essence of light. In great joy and ecstasy, Christopher sat down in the cave and realized that the king had known all along that this was the true purpose of this journey. With that understanding, he began laughing harder and longer than he had ever laughed before. By honoring the king's request above all else, an inner transformation had occurred within him, and he could now lead his brothers and sisters back to the kingdom.

We must face and rise above our greatest fear to fully awaken from this world of illusion. Yes, I am saying that every soul who has ever walked the earth is a God-realized being in the making. The duration of this process is unique to each individual, but in the end we will all come to the full realization that **in reality,**

we are all God. The only fear and barrier that keeps us from realizing the truth of who we are is the ego. The whole purpose and fulfillment of the spiritual journey is to voluntarily relinquish the false ego.

When Christopher returned with his brothers and sisters, they were all lovingly greeted by the king and all the subjects and the greatest of all feasts was held in their honor.

I have written this book with the intention of reaching all true spiritual seekers. Each of the twelve warriors represents an aspect of the lightworker's journey. Initially, they got lost in the darkness and enticements of the world. They eventually reach the Christopher stage and are ready to fulfill the purpose for which they initially entered the journey of duality. They are ready to live their lives as a living prayer.

I will explain the symbolism and purpose of the journey of lightworkers, represented by the twelve warriors, in much greater detail in a later chapter. The main point I want to make with this story is that our greatest prayer to God is reflected in the way we live our lives.

There was nothing wrong with the eleven other warriors choosing to go in different directions. There are many beautiful facets and many different paths to travel on Earth, but when one is ready to go all the way, the spiritual path is very simple and yet that simplicity translates into the symbolism of the crucifixion: **the voluntary relinquishment of the ego.** One who can follow this path directly up the mountain will be a light unto all who would follow. As Jeshua said, "I am the way, the truth, and the life" (John 14:6). Jeshua manifested that which he was teaching. In the same way, our actions must be in alignment with our prayers if we are to make progress on our spiritual journey. Ralph Waldo Emerson summed this up very nicely in his saying, "What you do speaks so loud, that I cannot hear what you say."

However you pray to God, make sure that you ask that His Will be done in your life. Seeking His Will places your life in the hands of perfection in which no error or failure is possible. Remember that in asking that God's Will be done, you are, in reality, asking that your own Will be done. **You are God.** I cannot emphasize this too many times as the ego will do everything in its power to convince you that it is blasphemy to even entertain such a ridiculous idea.

Suppose the captain of a ship was lost in a vast ocean with storms battering his ship on a daily basis and he had no idea which direction to take to get home. He sends out an SOS call and receives a reply from a lighthouse on the coast and is given direction on how to get home. This is exactly what true prayer does. It connects us with a spiritual beacon that will most assuredly bring us home. You may not believe it in the beginning, but if you seek God's Will in all you do, your faith will continue to grow until you begin to experience the Light within you that shall set you free.

Because of the efforts and spiritual awakenings of many of our brothers and sisters in the past and present, a new spiritual age has dawned upon this world. This is the beginning of a new age that will only get brighter as time goes by. I feel that this was the significance of the date December 21, 2012. I believe that this was a demarcation point in which the positive energy in the world began to outweigh the negative. One person with a high level of consciousness counterbalances millions of souls that are calibrating very low in consciousness. In this you can see how much more powerful the light is than the darkness.

Many who walk the spiritual path find that things are more difficult in the beginning of their journey. Others encounter severe tests after they have been on the path for a while. In the story, Christopher was willing to face his greatest fears because of his love and devotion to his king. He had to travel the last part of the journey all alone, which is what each of us will have to do on our spiritual journey. **No one but ourselves can really know what we are experiencing during this last phase.** All aspirants on the spiritual journey will, at one point or another, encounter initiations that are known as the "Dark Night of the Soul." This is not a test that God places in front of us to see if we are worthy or not. It is we who test ourselves. It usually happens that the stronger and more dedicated the soul, the more challenging the test. If we can use these difficult periods as an opportunity to let go of everything that is not real, we will experience a great awakening. In this process we are doing a great service to all who would follow after us. We will be opening spiritual portals that will make it much easier for those who follow after us, just as the early pioneers made it much easier for those who followed after them. Our lives then become a manifestation of the Way, the Truth, and the Life. Our lives will then reflect the essence of what a true living prayer is.

Surrendering to the Will of God is the highest prayer a soul can make because it is surrendering the false ego so that we can awaken to who we

truly are. When a soul truly realizes that his way of doing things has only brought him pain and futility, he will begin to seek something different. As long as we are dependent on our personal will to direct our lives, we will continue to experience the darkness of this world because our personal will is the ego's will. The ego's will only wants us to go into further darkness. At some point, we need to let go of our way of doing things and let God take over. In the Bible it states that God's strength is made perfect in our weakness (2 Corinthians 12). What this is saying is that when we recognize that our personal will has not taken us to where we want to go and it never will, then we will naturally surrender to God's Will and our weakness will be transformed into unlimited strength.

As a person nears the end of her journey and is very close to total transformation, she will find that there is no need to question anything. The reason for this is that she will know absolutely that God's Will and hers are one and the same. Therefore, everything—and I mean *everything*—that takes place in her life is a living prayer. What need is there to question anything?

One of the ego's last-ditch attempts to prevent a person from breaking free is to pose questions that could bring doubt to the individual, or pose a question that has no reasonable answer such as, "How could a perfect Son of God experience such pain and darkness?" At this stage of development, the aspirant simply ignores these questions with the statement, **"I question nothing because I trust in God completely."** (By the way, there is an answer to the ego's question that I will expand on later in the book.) The ego will try and keep us trapped in duality, but the ego is no match for the Will of God. There is no greater realization a person can have than to realize that her will and the Will of God are the same. When a person fully realizes this truth, through great effort on her part, she is totally free. Even though the person may not yet have fully awakened, there is an absolute assurance that the glorious event will soon take place. It's sort of like somebody in prison who has been paroled and is simply waiting for the paperwork to be completed before he can walk out of the prison gates to freedom. This state of assurance will surely come as we sincerely and persistently seek God's Will in our lives.

What if a soul is not ready to fully relinquish their will to God?

There is no judgment if we are not yet ready to go all the way. We do not pick an apple from a tree when it first appears as a bud. We need to wait until it ripens and is ready to eat before picking it. In the same way, a soul whose ego is not fully developed would not be ready to relinquish their personal will. In Chapter 3 of Ecclesiastes it states, "To everything there is a season and a time to every purpose under Heaven" (Ecclesiastes 3). The ego must be developed to a certain point before the spiritual journey can begin. On our spiritual journey it is very important not to judge anyone for anything they do or do not do because in our judgments we are confining ourselves to the realm of illusion. Each soul is creating their own experiences on this journey and each soul must face the consequences of what they are creating, whether the results are pleasant or difficult. Seek only to be a light on the path to others by living in a way that you become an example to others.

I will end this chapter with a funny story involving prayer that I heard many years ago...

There was a preacher giving a sermon when a tremendous rainstorm hit the town. The rain came down in buckets and it wasn't long before the church started to flood and the congregation left the church, but the preacher continued to preach. Soon the water was ankle-deep, and a man came by in a car and yelled to the preacher to get in the car but the preacher refused, saying, "I'm not worried, God will take care of me," and continued to preach even though the church was empty. When the water reached knee high, a man on a raft came by and yelled to the preacher to get on the raft before he drowned, but again the preacher yelled back that God would take care of him and kept on preaching. Then the water was waist high, and a man came by in a power boat and pleaded with the preacher to get in, but the preacher again said he was not afraid and that God would take care of him, so the boat left. It wasn't long before the water was neck high and a helicopter hovered over the church and a man yelled to the preacher that he better come out now or he would drown, but the preacher yelled back that God would take care of him and so the helicopter flew away. The water then got so deep that the preacher was sucked under the water and drowned. When he opened his eyes, he was in Heaven and immediately saw God and said, "Oh God, why didn't you save me from that horrible flood?" God replied, "I sent you a car, a raft, a power boat, and a helicopter but you did not pay any attention. What else did you want me to do?"

We are always receiving nudges and insights to lead us out of the darkness of illusion toward the Light of Understanding. We just need to trust in our prayers, have a little willingness and common sense.

Reflection Nine

True prayer is not only determined by us sitting quietly and talking to God. That is only a part of prayer. True prayer is also, maybe even more importantly, the way we live our daily lives and how we consciously think on a moment-by-moment basis. We have to ask ourselves about how we feel about the people around us. These feelings are also a form of prayer, whether it be a positive prayer or a negative prayer. Your every thought is a prayer so ask yourself, what are you putting out there in the universe as your prayer to God on a moment-by-moment basis? "Be it unto me according to your will Mother/Father God," is a perfect prayer if a person is truly willing to let go and let God take control of his life. The purpose of the spiritual journey is to reach a point in which every thought and action is a reflection of the Will of God. This is true prayer. Give some deep thought to this idea as it is a great light on the spiritual path.

Seeking His Will places your life in the hands of perfection in which no error or failure is possible. Talk from your heart and be sincere. Surrendering our individual will to the "One Will" that governs all, is a prayer to our own Divine Nature.

Ten

The Death of Illusion

As a deeper understanding and realization of who we are begins to settle into our consciousness, we begin to move into stage four of our spiritual journey.

Stage four is when the consciousness of our heart begins to direct our life. This is the stage of **Becoming** in which we not only know the Truth, we are the Truth. At this stage, we are a manifested blessing to the world because of the powerful love and light that we spread wherever we go.

Before this can happen, there is a slow eroding of the self we believed we were. This will be very frightening to the false ego as its very nature is being threatened. When a soul reaches this final stage, many will turn around as the identification with the false self is still too embedded in the consciousness and the fear of losing who they think they are becomes extremely frightening to the ego. It truly is a death of the false "I" and only those who are courageous and who desire the Truth above all else will be able to continue on the miraculous journey into the knowing that **you are One with God and are God.** There are many stages to the spiritual journey before a soul will face this ultimate death of the illusionary ego, so if you are not ready to enter this final gate, that is perfectly alright. There is absolutely no time frame for a soul to return to the Godhood that they are. So do not feel pressured if you are not ready for this final step. Just know that you are perfect exactly as you are and where you are.

It wasn't until after the death of Linda, my partner of twenty-nine years, that I was able to enter stage four of my journey. I felt like my heart was ripped open after her departure. It was only then that I had access to the deeper facets of my heart and could allow my heart to take over as the director of my path. I experienced so many beautiful feelings and frequencies emanating from my heart during this time. My relationships with others became much more pleasant and joyous as my heart was now in charge of my life.

The greatest barrier that almost all souls on Earth have is their identification with their thoughts and beliefs. I am now going to say something that will be strongly resisted by the ego. **You are not your thoughts, nor even the thinker of your thoughts.** As long as a person identifies with their thoughts and beliefs, they will remain caught up in the prison of illusion.

If I am not my thoughts or even the thinker of my thoughts, then who am I?

This lack of understanding is the dilemma that is keeping most people tied to the prison of illusion. Your thoughts and beliefs are like turning your radio station to a certain channel. If you are dwelling on thoughts of sadness, then you are tuning into the frequency of sadness, which is part of the world consciousness. If your thoughts are on lack of wealth, then you are tuning into the frequency of that channel of the world consciousness. You asked who you would be if you were not your thoughts or even the thinker of your thoughts. **You are the observer of your thoughts and everything that seems to be happening in the world, without any judgment or interpretation of what is taking place.** This practice of being the observer, rather than identifying with your thoughts or what appears to be happening, will eventually lead to the dissolution of the false ego and the false belief in who we thought we were. It will lead you to the death of the false self or ego, which has kept you separated from God or your True Self. It will also bring you the greatest joy, peace and love you could ever possibly imagine.

One of the greatest challenges to the dissolution of the false self is the powerful influence of the world mind on a person. In this world, the desire for wealth and recognition are two of the most difficult illusions to overcome.

There is nothing wrong with wanting wealth unless it becomes a barrier to your spiritual awakening. Wealth can be a very big obstacle to the Divine Love, Joy and Peace of our true nature. In fact, many people with great wealth are often the least satisfied with life because of the realization that everything they have does not bring them true happiness. Money can bring distractions to how you are truly feeling but not lasting happiness. Eventually, all souls will finally come to the realization that the only thing that can bring true fulfillment on Earth is the awakening to the realization of who they truly are. A single mother living paycheck to paycheck, who has come to this spiritual realization, is infinitely richer than a Wall Street tycoon counting his shares. When a person is born, they encounter circumstances that best suit the karma they agreed to experience and to learn from. These karmic influences can create much confusion and short-circuit the information coming from our heart, so that we only hear the information coming from the brain. When we reach stage four of our spiritual journey, we then begin to hear and understand very clearly what our heart is saying and directing us to do.

In this final stage, we have cleared the way for the heart to take its rightful place as the director of our lives. Our thoughts and feelings and actions will then be in accordance with spiritual truth. It doesn't mean that we have reached a state of Full Spiritual Enlightenment. It means that the way has been cleared for us to reach this holy state without all the interference we were dealing with before this time.

Reaching stage four doesn't mean we cannot fall back to one of the earlier stages. It really depends on our willingness to truly listen to and follow the dictates of the heart, which is the same as listening to our higher self. We will probably still have a lot of issues to deal with at this stage, but we will not identify with them as much. Eventually, we will know that in reality we are perfectly innocent and always have been. At this point we are starting to transcend the world. We will have the full realization that the ego never existed and that **we are Spirit in Union with God who is everything that is and that will ever be.** The power of the light emanating from an enlightened soul has a tremendous impact on the mind of the world and accelerates the transformation process of mankind.

The final outcome of stage four is the manifestation of a fully developed spiritual soul. It is at this stage that the individual has fully developed spiritually. This is the spiritual development Jeshua manifested in his life as the Christ 2,000 years ago. This final stage must be preceded by the death of the individual false ego.

During my spiritual journey, I have had a few spiritual insights that gave me an understanding of what it would be like at the death of my personal ego. One of the first ones happened just as I was waking up one morning about twelve years ago. I was shown how my final spiritual awakening was to take place. As I was lying in bed ready to get up, I heard a very clear voice say to me, "This is the way your spiritual awakening will take place." In an extremely clear vision, I saw myself walking across a room when all of a sudden, a huge burst of brilliant white light exploded within me and the person I believed I had been was completely gone. There was nothing in the past to hold on to, nothing of Gil to relate to. In Gil's place was an infinite consciousness so vast and powerful that at the time it was a little scary because of the enormous sudden change. In the years that followed, I had many powerful spiritual experiences that supported my greater insights into this final step of my spiritual journey. There is nothing to fear; this realization will only happen when a person is fully ready to relinquish the false "I."

Another one of these experiences happened on December 8, 2012. It was a very brief dream that was so powerful that I immediately woke up and could not go back to sleep. It happened at about 1:30 in the morning. Even though the dream only lasted a very short time, I experienced the death of me as an individual in such a real way that it actually felt like I had died. I actually experienced what it felt like to take a quick last breath before death. The big difference was that I was not experiencing the death of the body, but rather the annihilation of my individuality. After lying in bed for an hour contemplating the experience of the death of my individuality, I realized I would not be able to go back to sleep. I got dressed and had a cup of tea as I continued to go over the short, but powerful dream. I then turned on the computer and began writing this new chapter. These two experiences, plus a number of other ego death experiences I've had, showed me very clearly the futility of holding on to my separate identity.

A soul can still fulfill his spiritual purpose, without the death of the ego, if they are not quite ready for this final step. There will come a lifetime when the death of our individual ego will occur but there is no time limit for this to happen.

It sounds like there is an element of control on our part. Is the awakening experience something we can help along, or not?

The control we have is what we do with the temporary realization that is presented to us. It's up to us to act on this realization while acknowledging the role Grace plays in this great endeavor.

All beings will eventually experience the death of the ego. Here on Earth, the third dimension is so much denser than any other planet that the opportunity is greater to face the ego and go through the transformation process.

There are also different levels of awakening and different gifts that come with the different awakenings. For instance, there are also many spiritual teachers that still identify with the ego. However, **as long as the ego is identified with, there is always the possibility of falling from Grace.**

When I was in priest class in the Holy Order of MANS, one of the exercises given to us by Father Paul was to see how long we could carry on conversations without using the word "I." Some of my fellow students and I would make a game of it and maybe bet a cup of coffee on who could go the longest without saying "I." I was surprised at how quickly I used the word "I." I didn't do very well in the game. I was still very attached, at that time, to my individual sense of identity.

At this time, many people are having awakening experiences. There is a large awakening taking place, even amongst some who were not even interested in spirituality. Some awakenings are temporary and some are permanent. The one thing that is constant in all true awakenings, whether temporary or permanent, is that there is a realization that this world and the individuality we have identified with are not real.

In awakening, we may lose our identification with and attachment to the individuality we have identified with, but we will always have a uniqueness that is different from any other soul ever created. As I stated before, this is the **I AM THAT I AM** within us that can never be lost or die.

I know why I chose this very difficult path, and I am totally grateful for all the help I have received along the way. The final part of my spiritual journey was like being in a boat on a river with no paddles and the boat is being carried by the current of the river. The journey on the river was not all calm and smooth as there were still many rapids that I passed through along the way. I had no idea where the current was taking me, I just knew that where I was at each moment was exactly where I was supposed to be. Toward the end, I had surrendered so completely that there was no resistance to anything that happened, whether pleasant or unpleasant, I simply observed them without judgment or interpretation. I enjoyed the pleasant parts of the journey and I learned from the unpleasant experiences. The unpleasant experiences were there to reveal to me that there were still attachments to the illusionary self which still needed resolution and dissolving.

We are in a time of monumental change and chaos in the world. There is also tremendous upheaval going on within the minds and emotions of most souls on the planet at this time, including many on the spiritual path. Many are going through the Dark Night of the Soul, which is part of the process of dying to the false ego. It is said that the darkest hour is just before dawn and in this case, it is literally true. Many are waking up from the illusion of this world to the great reality of who we really are. We are entering a period in which the Golden Dawn of Spiritual Awakening is taking place within individuals on a large scale. When this world was formed and first inhabited, it was literally Paradise. It will again be transformed into a paradise as we move through this glorious process of getting in touch with the truth within us. The Kingdom of Heaven is within each one of us. Believe it or not, there are many beings on the Other Side that would be happy to change places with you. Earth provides an incredible opportunity for experience and accelerated spiritual growth that a soul can find nowhere else in the universe.

St. Paul said in one of his letters to the Corinthians, "I die daily" (1 Corinthians 15:31). He was referring to a person's surrendering and dying to all the beliefs and identifications of his personal life. This death happens on a moment-by-moment basis so that a person can be reborn into the truth of who he truly is. The journey to spiritual awakening is difficult but it is not complicated.

As I mentioned earlier, when God created the souls and gave us free will, anything became possible. The illusory world we made up seemed to appear because of our desire to experience life separate from God. To make this possible, our ego seemed to come into being as a character on the screen of life. This dream consists of nothing but a false belief system. What appears on the screen of life is determined by our beliefs, desires and will. None of the screen characters are real. They are simply part of our dream scenario. As our spiritual understanding develops, we gain more insight over what appears on the screen of our mind. At some point in our individual movie we enter the dying process of our own personal ego, and this is where our personal illusory movie ends, very happily, I must say.

Many years ago, I had the inspiration to perform a ceremony in which I would burn personal pictures of me and others close to me, as my expression of my willingness to fully relinquish the illusion of Gil. I invited my partner Ashleigh to witness this process. She was disturbed when she saw her photo included in this step but simultaneously on a higher level also understood this spiritual process I needed to experience. When I started the ceremony, I was amazed at the tremendous emotion I was experiencing. I could hardly get a couple of words out of my mouth at a time because of the emotion that filled my whole body. What was happening is that the part of the ego that still existed in me was going through a sort of death process. At this juncture, I knew I was ready to embody the much deeper truth of who we really are.

I mentioned having a very powerful experience in a two-day intensive with Muktananda in New York. Immediately after his touch, in a very clear vision, I opened my eyes and saw in both my open hands a caterpillar-like creature with a tail of a rattlesnake. I was startled by this vision and I automatically threw it off my right hand! I then realized there was a very strong significance to this experience, so I was more careful about the caterpillar-like creature that I held in my left hand. A Priestess with long dark hair, wearing a blue robe, approached me while I was sitting in my chair and carefully removed the creature from my left hand while gently cuffing it into her hand. She then walked carefully to the back of the room and took it behind a dark blue curtain. Initially, there was a dislike toward her but as she walked away holding the creature, my heart opened into the deepest love for her. As she walked away, I received that she was symbolic of the number 3. This was a very powerful premonition of Ashleigh coming into my life and supporting me through all my spiritual endeavors. It would be over thirty years before we actually met in the physical. I was visiting Sedona when I was first introduced to her and there was an immediate soul recognition. I later learned that my former partner Linda, who is one of my spirit guides, had orchestrated our meeting. In numerology the number 3 was significant to Ashleigh's soul.

I realized she was the Priestess I had seen in my premonition with Muktananda. There were many powerful synchronicities throughout my relationship with Ashleigh and we have supported each other through tremendous growth and soul expansion.

I realized that throwing off this creature in my right hand meant that I wasn't consciously ready to integrate what was yet to come into my being. At the time I couldn't consciously hold it, so I threw it off. Ashleigh then took the responsibility to take care of the creature in my left hand until I was ready. The left hand symbolizes the subconscious which needs time to integrate.

This is indicative of how God works through me and directs me in all things, as my will is aligned with the Will of God in the act of total surrender. Everything is laid out for me and requires no effort on my part. Through my faith and knowing, everything simply flows.

I have mentioned many times that in order to find our true self, we must die to the illusion that we have created over many, many lifetimes. This is a total experience of utter surrender. Surrender opens the way for Grace to direct our process. These lifetimes have been experienced on many planes and dimensions. These lifetimes and experiences have gone on to make up the identity of that which we think we are. It's only the fear of losing our egoic self that keeps a soul from experiencing our true nature, which is the awareness and acceptance of the infinite consciousness that we are destined to have when we merge with God.

Our Union with God is so completely fearful to the ego that most souls are not even able to begin conceiving of such a state, much less being able to embody such a thought. Yet as hard as it is to accept, this is the truth of who we are and which will be experienced by all at some distant point in the so-called future. Everyone will reach a state of consciousness in which they will be able to fully accept this truth.

Escaping from the illusion of this world can be likened to a person in the theater getting out of his chair, turning his back on the screen of illusion and walking out into the bright sunlight of reality. In order to do this, he must give up his identification with everything on the screen of unreality. This is the death of the ego. When a person leaves the theater of illusion, he will see life as it truly is in all its glory, love, joy, peace and beauty. After his awakening, he can walk back into the theater, bringing the light of wisdom with him in order to help others to also escape the theater of illusion and death. As we leave the theater of illusion, we experience the pure joy and reality of who we are and the unity of all life.

The process of awakening may seem to take a long time, but it depends on how dedicated we are to knowing the truth and our willingness to die to the illusion. There is so much spiritual light entering Earth right now that the process of awakening has really taken on an accelerated pace for those who are ready for the truth. We just have to be willing to let go of the illusions and beliefs that keep us confined to the dream.

Be patient and persistent. Patience was one of the most difficult lessons I had to learn. I was like the majority of people who always wanted things to happen immediately. This is an attitude that is very prevalent in America and around the world. Look at all the fast-food restaurants, drive through cleaners and a myriad of other institutions that provide instant gratification to the masses. The path to awakening is a process in the consciousness that does seem to take some time, but the final result is absolutely assured.

In the 1960s, Timothy Leary, the LSD guru, had a saying: "Turn on, tune in and drop out." He was trying to get people to open their eyes to all the greed and corruption of those in power. By recommending that people take LSD, he was hoping that they would see that those in power were trying to give us a blueprint on how our lives should be lived in order to be successful. His message was that the success the world was preaching simply led to emptiness and finally, death. Mr. Leary was on the right track, but his methods could only take a person so far and unfortunately many who traveled that path wound up very dysfunctional.

We have never done anything wrong, we are totally innocent and have always been. If we can fully accept this truth, we won't be afraid to meet God face to face, which is the same as facing our True Self. Think of the one person you love more than anybody in the whole world. Now imagine that you have been separated from this person for ten years. Imagine how happy you would be to be reunited with this person. Our reunification with God will be experienced with unimaginable joy. Many of us may feel that we are not pure enough to meet with God because of what the world has programmed us to believe about ourselves. Underneath all the false concepts, judgments and beliefs we have about ourselves, each one of us is totally pure and holy. **We not only deserve to meet with God, each one of us is a unique part of God. We are God walking upon Earth,** so how much more deserving are we of everything that is?

Don't be afraid when the ego starts to go through its death throes. This is not *your* death, but rather the beginning of your rebirth into the Glory of God. It is only an illusion, which dies. I mentioned several times before that once the ego becomes aware of your efforts to free yourself from its clutches, it will get very upset and try everything to stop you from seeing the truth. Remember this when you are going through difficult times. **Observe what is happening in you without judging it in any way.**

One of the great mistakes a soul makes when entering this path of dissolving the ego is the identification with the pain of the dying ego, instead of simply being a witness to this dying process. Witnessing without identification is a precious spiritual tool to use in your journey into enlightenment. Difficult times are opportunities to learn more about ourselves and the ego.

One thing I still don't understand is that you speak of the ego as a thing that does exist and on the other hand, you say it does not exist. How can it be both ways?

In this world of dreams and illusion, the ego *does* seem to exist because we believe it is who we are. Understand that even though this world does not exist in reality, it does exist in the minds of people who are caught up in illusion. Because we are children of God, our beliefs have great power regardless of whether the belief is based on illusion or reality. Jeshua said, "Be it unto you as you believe" (Matthew 8:13). Illusion does not affect the realm of reality or God, but it unfortunately seems to have an effect on the believer. As long as we believe in duality of any kind, the ego will exist in our mind. At some point in creation, all illusions will disappear from our mind as if it had never been there.

All the forces in Heaven and Earth are at your beck and call once you truly make up your mind to return to God. There are many who are in a physical body at this time who have come to help the masses of people during this time of great opportunity. Don't be deceived by all the darkness that is prevalent in the world today. Many things will happen in the next few years that will be very confusing to the masses. We completed a 26,000-year cycle, which culminated on December 21, 2012. At the end of a cycle, there are always old things that need to be discarded to make way for the new. This process is now taking place on many levels. The energies and opportunities to awaken are now more available to us than at any other time because of the age we live in.

The TV series *The X-Files* always ended with the saying, "The truth is out there." Well, the truth is **within each of us and is totally available to anyone who has the courage to seek it.** The happiness we all crave is at hand. I only pray that the hearts and minds of all mankind will be open to receive this Grace. God bless you all with His perfect Love, Light and Strength as you walk the holy path. I speak to you as a humble brother and servant.

Reflection Ten

The most difficult process a soul will ever have to encounter is literally the crucifixion of the false self which we believe and think we are. The great majority of people on Earth at this time are not ready to even conceive of such a death because they fully believe they are the egoic self.

The one thing that is constant in all true awakenings, whether temporary or permanent, is that there is a realization that this world and the individuality we have identified with are not real. People may have an awakening and an opening, but the opening can close if they don't act on that powerful opportunity of recognizing what once was considered real, is not real; and what was considered truth, is actually false.

If this opening is not acknowledged and acted upon, the expanded consciousness will contract again, like a window opening and shutting, resulting in a temporary awakening, as opposed to a permanent awakening. It's up to us as to whether we act on and value this temporary realization or we just allow it to be another experience that we put in our memory storage.

Know that there will come a time when every soul will pass through the process of the death of the I. It could be many lifetimes before a soul reaches the point of being willing and ready for this final death of the ego. Be patient with yourself.

Eleven

Forgiving the Illusion

In reality, forgiveness is an illusion because in truth we have never done anything wrong. Through our insane idea of believing we could separate ourselves from God, we created the impossible. We created a place that does not, nor could, ever exist. God is all there is, and God is Pure Unconditional Love. This illusionary world is definitely not a place where unconditional love reigns, except through those who have become enlightened. Fortunately, we are in an age where many are now Awakening.

Are you saying we really don't need to forgive ourselves or others because forgiveness is an illusion?

Forgiveness is a valuable and necessary tool to use on our way to enlightenment, even though it is an illusion. Without forgiveness, we couldn't get very far on the spiritual journey. Forgiveness propels you on a path to the gates of Heaven but cannot get you into the Kingdom. Before you can enter into a state of Union with God, a soul must have completely released the belief in the false egoic self.

A very difficult lesson for me to embody on my spiritual journey was self-forgiveness. I was always my harshest critic and felt like I had to be perfect or I was a failure. Perfection in the realm of duality is an illusion and so I was trying to live up to an impossible concept of what I thought I needed to be. I can remember that as far back as a child of three I was striving for a state of perfection. Little did I know that this striving to be perfect was actually a barrier to reaching the state of freedom and Oneness that I so longed for, because I was trying to make the ego perfect, which, in reality, does not exist. During the first thirty years of my spiritual journey in this life, I crucified myself internally whenever I believed I had made mistakes. This attitude created intense stress in my body and a severe restriction and fear in my ability to fully relate with others.

At one point, the fear and tension that I experienced when relating to groups caused a real problem in my life and I was intent on finding out the cause. The only thing I knew for sure was that this fear began a very short time after joining the Holy Order of MANS. I wanted so badly to find out the cause of this fear and tension that I made an appointment to see a hypnotherapist. I was thinking that the cause came from the traumas that filled my childhood. The hypnotherapist induced a state of deep relaxation in me and told me to get in touch with the fear and tension and to use that as a vehicle to go back to the initial cause of this state of unease. I got in touch with the fear and very clearly saw myself going back in time to being a child, and then into another lifetime where I saw myself in a tunic and sandals. I saw that I was a spiritual leader in that life and had a large following. The people in power at that time were only seeking more power for themselves and were not doing the people's will, so at one point I encouraged my followers to overthrow the existing establishment and many died in the process of the rebellion. The rebellion was successful and I was put in power. By this time I was so remorseful and critical of myself for what I felt was an abuse of my position as a spiritual guide that I withdrew from public life and faded into the background. I lived the final years of that life in a state of deep seclusion and remorse. In this hypnotic state, I was then shown a number of lives that immediately followed that lifetime and in each one, I was a monk who lived a very austere and penitent life. I literally crucified myself for having believed that I made this mistake as a spiritual leader. I now understand why I felt I had to be perfect and why I was so critical of myself in this life for any mistake I made as I did not want to repeat the mistakes of the past.

If there are only a few ideas in this book that a person fully understands and consistently uses in their daily life, then I hope one of them is forgiveness. *True forgiveness* is one of our keys to liberation.

Can a person reach the state of awakening without forgiveness?

In the beginning of the journey home, it is pretty clear that forgiveness is absolutely necessary to move toward enlightenment. Forgiveness opens our spiritual sight and allows us to experience that our innocence was never lost. This realization opens the door to our awakening. Forgiving and loving ourselves is the simplest and easiest way to allow the light into our minds.

The way we want to approach forgiveness is to forgive yourself and others for anything we are conscious of. We don't need to worry about our unconscious guilt. If there is a need for the unconscious guilt in us to be brought to our conscious awareness, it will happen at the perfect time. The Holy Spirit will help us in releasing the guilt we are unaware of, as long as we forgive what we are aware of.

True forgiveness must come from the heart in order for it to be effective. We should practice forgiving ourselves and others for every negative thought, feeling, and action. This includes those little irritations and impatience. Eventually, forgiveness will allow enough Light into our being, allowing us to realize we have never done anything for which we need to be forgiven. Eventually, the full realization dawns in our minds that the individual we thought we were in fact never existed. I know I have mentioned this fact many times, but this is the last hurdle a soul will have to cross to realize that their separation from God indeed never happened. In the meantime, keep forgiving.

We should forgive ourselves for any pain or sickness we experience because those symptoms are a manifestation of some guilt or fear in our mind. In my spiritual journey, I forgave myself for anything that created discomfort in my life, including something like a slight headache. If I had a headache I would say or think something like this to myself: **"I forgive myself completely for whatever guilt or false belief there is in my mind that caused the headache. Yet as I forgive myself for whatever the seeming cause is, I know that I am forgiving myself for an illusion, for a bad dream I am having and I forgive the dreamer of this dream."** You can shorten your statement of forgiveness or substitute anything for a headache. Change the wording as you like but always remain faithful to the premise of true forgiveness. It is extremely important to remember that we are forgiving ourselves or others for something that never actually happened. It's a dream and a dream only. Forgive, forgive, and then forgive some more.

The keys to Awakening are contained in the understanding of what forgiveness really means. I hope that after reading this chapter you will have an understanding of what true forgiveness is.

The forgiveness that many religions practice is based on a good principle but it won't set us free because it is based on the belief that a person has committed sins and is guilty. This type of forgiveness supports the belief that sin is real. **We all make mistakes in our worldly journey, but as we develop spiritually it is our responsibility to learn from those mistakes. Mistakes can be corrected, but letting go of the illusion of sin is more difficult. True forgiveness is based on the understanding that we are forgiving ourselves and others for a false belief, a dream and nothing more.**

When we sincerely start to walk the spiritual path, the ego will be very quick to judge and condemn us for any little thing that we appear to do wrong. If we are not vigilant about the ego's underhanded tactics, we will find ourselves believing the ego and thus join it in judging and condemning ourselves and others. Judging and condemning ourselves is a pitfall that just about all of us on the path fall into many times. **We think we are being righteous by condemning ourselves for any wrongs we think we have done. This is one of the main tricks the ego uses to keep us from the truth. It is extremely important not to let ourselves fall into the trap of self-condemnation.**

Are you saying we can do anything we want as long as we don't judge or condemn ourselves for the action?

First of all, it is not you creating the act, it is only your belief and identification with the action that causes judgment or condemnation. Only if you are enlightened would you be able to act without any judgment because enlightened beings know that whatever energy is manifesting through them is in perfect accord with the Will of God. To be enlightened is to be in the Pure Light of God, which is one with Unconditional Love. Unconditional love acts in a way which is always for the best and highest of any individual.

There is a facet of the ego that is very important for us to understand if we are going to begin using true forgiveness. **The ego encourages us to project our guilt onto others. This act of projection does not relieve us of our guilt, but it does seem to bring relief for a short while. Projection comes in many forms, but it is always for the purpose of relieving ourselves of our inner guilt.** We then seek to avoid the pain and anxiety that comes from the feeling of guilt in us by projecting it onto others. The majority of the world practices projection in one form or another.

How many countless times when we are feeling bad do we find some exterior person or situation to blame for our problems? If we take a close look at ourselves the next time we blame or condemn someone else, we will find that we feel a little bit better or self-righteous for the time being. We may actually feel downright good. The reason for this is that we seem to be projecting some of our inner guilt onto some other person, place, or thing in order to relieve some of that pressure inside ourselves. **The problem is that there is no other person, place, or thing. This is our dream and our dream only. Everybody and everything in our dream is a part of ourselves and that is why it is so important to forgive others, because by forgiving others we are literally forgiving ourselves.**

It's interesting that psychiatrists and psychologists will tell us that all the people in our dreams are an aspect of our own personality. It's the same thing with our everyday waking dream. Everything is happening in our mind. So we can project as much as we want, but this will not lessen our pain because the pain will still remain within us. We are simply projecting it onto a seemingly separated part of our mind, which we will eventually have to face.

The projection of guilt is very clearly played out in our political system. It seems that the politician who does a better job in blaming their opponent for this or that is usually the one who gets elected. The predominant two-party political system in America is an ideal situation in which the ego can use the tool of projection to create animosity and separation between people. The projection game is also frequently played out in the parent and child relationship as well as the partnership relationship, where this projection seems to be a natural part of life.

To blame another for our condition in life is like Joe blaming the delivery boy for delivering the ice cream Joe himself ordered. Joe knew before he ordered it that he was allergic to dairy and yet he still insisted on ordering it and then blamed somebody else for his allergic reaction. So, the delivery boy became his scapegoat.

One of the most difficult ego traps that we have to understand is the act of comparing ourselves to others. The whole world revolves around competition and being better than our neighbors. This is the nature of duality. The cure for the disease of comparison and competition is the realization that we are all one. Only when we can look through the eyes of forgiveness can we see each other as we truly are. When we stop looking through the eyes of duality, we naturally forgive whatever we are judging. We no longer compare. An enlightened mind sees no difference or separation between himself and others. Spiritual knowledge opens the door to true forgiveness, which reveals the oneness of all things.

If we were to have access to the moment-by-moment thoughts of the great majority of people, we would become aware that almost one hundred percent of their thoughts are ego directed. Just about all thoughts in this world are based on the assumption that we are individuals and separate from everyone else.

It is not an easy task to dissolve the illusion of the ego, but it can and must be done if we are to fully awaken spiritually. We must become spiritual warriors to break free of the illusionary ropes that the ego uses to keep us bound. **Guilt is one of the ego's strongest weapons to keep us asleep. The tool to dissolve guilt is Forgiveness.** No one is guilty of anything because everything that we experience is happening in a dream we are having. There is really nobody else out there. We are the creator and the witness of everything that happens in our life. The power is in our hands and we can choose to change what seems to appear in our lives, or we can go on blindly believing that we are victims of the world. The only true change or transformation takes place in our mind.

The essence of Truth lies in the understanding that we are One with God and have never done anything wrong. We have just been having a dream from which we must awaken and forgiveness will bring about that awakening.

Our Oneness with God has nothing to do with our bodies, our individuality, or this world. **Our Oneness with God is the result of waking up to the reality That All Things Are God.** Our ego does not want us to realize this Truth. Spiritual light dissolves the illusion of the ego. When a person is truly ready to begin the process of dissolving their ego, forgiveness will help accelerate this spiritual process.

Forgiveness begins a process of removing the layers of film that have covered our true sight. The more egoic layers we remove through our forgiveness efforts, the more light is available to us. The more light we have, the more we remember the truth of who we truly are. We are aware that without light we cannot see what is happening in this physical world and yet even on the brightest of days, what we see with our physical eyes has nothing to do with reality. Our vision and perspective is completely distorted because our physical eyes only relay to our brain pictures, sounds, and feelings of an illusionary world. Spiritual light is very different from ordinary light. To see with spiritual vision is to see the truth behind the veil of illusion.

A fully awakened individual may appear to be in the world, but is in no way attached to it. This may shed some light on the statement made by Jeshua, **"I am in the world, but not of it"** (John 17:14-16). Jeshua knew that the world was not real—that it was just a dream—but he came into this illusion to help us to awaken from the dream.

If what you are saying is true, why does it appear that we are all having the same dream? We all get similar information about world events.

This is because we all have an agreement to experience the world in the way we do. We might call this an agreement of the mass consciousness of the world and of each soul entering this dimension. We needed this agreement between each other to have some semblance of order in experiencing a dimension of duality with linear time and space. We experience Earth with the belief that we are separated so that we can each create our own reality from different perspectives. Therefore, we all share in a dream using our unique perspective to choose what our soul needs to experience. This determines what type of dream experience we will have. As I mentioned before, when an audience experiences a movie there will be many different feelings and perspectives about the movie, because of the different beliefs and emotional states within each of us. It's the same movie, and yet there will be many different reactions to the different characters and scenes.

We all seem to be looking at the same world, but how we see it depends on our state of consciousness. Just think what we could do if we all chose to see the world as a place of love and joy. What an amazing transformation of the world this would create in a very short time.

Our will is the determining factor as to when we will choose to awaken from this illusion. It is taking place in our mind, and it is in our mind where the choice and changes have to be made. When we make the choice to change, we activate the heart center, which is where God dwells within each of us. We must understand that our beliefs create a world of effects totally unique to the thinker. The cause is in the mind. What we believe is true, is true for us and that determines what we seem to experience.

Beliefs create a world of effects. If a person believed they are a victim, the effects of that belief would all line up to bring about circumstances in their life to support that belief. This is unique to each individual. **By the observation of the thoughts going through the mind, one can choose which thoughts to support and which thoughts not to give life to.**

If none of this really happened, then why do we need to forgive?

Because we believe it really happened. We are really forgiving our own false beliefs, our individual dream, and this is why we need to begin with self-forgiveness. Life on Earth is a dream and most of us have not forgiven ourselves for the dream we are having. Most souls, as of this date, are not yet ready to give up the dream of illusion and that is perfectly fine. We can continue in this sleep state as long as we desire. There is no time limit, nor is there any condemnation or judgment if that is our choice.

How can we help people who are suffering if we believe none of this is actually happening?

The truth is that none of this ever happened and we are living in a world that is not real. None of this ever happened. It is a conundrum that the egoic mind will never be able to understand.

I will use the analogy of watching a movie. This time I will liken us to the projectionist in the booth upstairs. Our mind is symbolic of a projectionist who projects his beliefs, desires, and fears on the screen of life. There are billions of projectionists and each one is projecting their own character on the screen. There is an agreement between all the projectionists to share in the same movie from their own personal perspective. Each projectionist believes that the movie on the screen is really happening. Now, suppose one of the projectionists wakes up and sees that the movie is just an illusion and is not really real. Through his awakened state, his character on the screen starts emanating a great deal of light, which begins affecting many of the other projectionists and many of them also start to awaken. This is how an enlightened being can affect so many without saying a word.

Have you ever been asleep and had somebody shine a bright light on your face? Unless you were in a very, very deep sleep, the light would awaken you. A spiritually awakened person will naturally allow his light to shine upon the world so that others may awaken. We are seeking to awaken the projectionist in the booth and not the character on the screen. It is the dreamer of the movie who needs to be awakened and not the dream character on the screen because that character is not real. Does this give you a better idea of how we can help others and still not give credence to this illusion?

A spiritually awakened person does not deny that others are going through a lot of suffering because she has been through her share of suffering. She understands that if she is to help others, she must have the realization that suffering cannot exist in Love/God and therefore it cannot be real. Our realization that it is not real is the only way we can truly help others. In quantum physics it has been discovered that there is nothing in this world that is real unless we observe it. It is our belief that seems to make things real in the illusionary realm of time. Outside the realm of illusion, there is only one Truth and that is Love. If we focus on the suffering of ourselves and others as real, we are giving life and power to those conditions and circumstances and thus we continue to make the dream real in our mind. We should have compassion for others and not pity. Pity validates the illusion. If we become a conscious observer of illusion, then that which is not real will eventually disappear and we'll be able to see clearly so that we can help those who are ready to receive it.

Jeshua said, "Greater love has no man than this, that he lays down his life for his friends" (John 15:13). What this statement does not reveal is that **the life we are laying down is the life of the illusionary ego**, which is causing us all our pain, depression, and separation. So as we forgive ourselves and surrender our personal ego, we are actually performing the greatest act of love for ourselves as well as for others.

Please don't think you are being uncaring of others by inwardly refusing to give credence to their pain. An enlightened person will have compassion for somebody in pain but will not empower the pain by believing in it, or giving reality to the situation, because in his eyes it is not real. Do you see the difference? If Jeshua had believed that the affliction in the person he was healing was real, he would not have been able to heal them. He saw the perfection in each person he was healing. True compassion is doing what is necessary to help others to free themselves from their guilt, without getting involved in the dream, which is the cause of pain. Equally important is to always have empathy.

The ego cannot exist without judgment. The very nature of the ego is to make a judgment about anything and everything. Don't make the mistake of missing the incredible depth and importance of this statement. In this world, judgment is as natural as breathing. Whenever we see somebody we know very well, we see that person with all sorts of preconceived opinions as to who they are. All the experiences we have had with them colors the way we perceive them. All these beliefs and feelings about the person perpetuate an illusionary image of that person in our mind. When we fully awaken, our perceptions of others will be transformed completely. The belief system of this world is the antithesis of the Truth. That is why spiritual aspirants have to question whether their belief system is helping them to awaken, or keeping them sound asleep. When a soul has laid aside all judgments, he is very near the door of full awakening.

How could anyone be expected not to have preconceived beliefs about people they know very well? Our perception of this world is made up of everything we have experienced in life, including our relationships and beliefs about others.

Here underlines the importance of striving to completely reverse the way we see the world. Seeing others you have known for years in a totally new way may sound difficult, but let me give you an analogy that will help in this process.

Imagine that a kindergarten class was putting on a show for Halloween. In the show, each child had a cardboard cutout of different ghouls and other scary images that they carried in front of them as they spoke their part. Everybody in the audience knew that behind the scary cutout was an innocent child. The audience would probably laugh and think the play was cute and would not be afraid of the cutouts. Similarly, an enlightened person sees a much different world than the masses of people.

People carry many, many different personas that they project out into the world. A person might project the identity of a thief, an executive, an actress, a homeless person, and many other projections. All of these images carry as much reality as the cutouts that the children carried in their Halloween play. These images have nothing to do with the soul that is behind these images. The image is only a temporary mask that the soul has put on. To see past these illusory images is to begin seeing with spiritual sight.

Over and over again we make decisions as to whether we choose to remain separated by choosing judgment, or seek to return to a state of unity by choosing forgiveness. The choice is ours and ours alone. The thought process of the ego is insane, so our choice is between insanity or sanity. Try to envision another person not as a physical body, but rather as a divine spirit, a child of God. This process takes practice and time, but as I stated before, the spiritual journey is beyond question the greatest and highest quest a person could possibly pursue. We can use time to continue the cycle of birth and death, or we can use time to wake up from this dream. It all depends on how we use our mind and our will while we are in a body.

If we practice seeing everything that happens in our life without judgment or resistance, we are well on our way to a new life. I will share a fictional story I heard many years ago that I hope will inspire you to accept whatever happens in your life without resistance:

Once there was a monk who lived in a small town in Japan. One of the unmarried women of the town became pregnant and the people of the town demanded to know who the father was. The woman wanted to protect her lover, so she told the people that the monk was the father. The people ran to the monk's hut and started yelling and cursing him. The monk did not deny the story and remaining very peaceful, he looked at the people and said, "Ah so." Several months later, when the woman had given birth to the child, the people of the town took the baby away from her and took it to the monk who they felt had the responsibility of raising the child. When the people saw the monk, they again cursed him for his evil deed and handed him the baby. He gently received the baby, looked at the people and said, "Ah so." After a couple of weeks, the mother of the baby could not bear to be without her child, so she told the people the truth about who the real lover was and that the couple planned on getting married. The people ran to the monk's hut and retrieved the baby and profusely apologized to the monk for their false accusations. The monk looked at them and simply replied, "Ah so."

It is difficult for most of us to refrain from judging somebody we don't like, even if they have not done anything to us personally. It is almost impossible for most of us not to project judgment on somebody when they have said or done something mean against us, with or without justification. The monk in the story represented somebody who knew perfectly well that nobody could hurt or judge him except himself. He didn't need to justify himself to an illusion. He accepted everything that happened to him with total peace because he knew who he was. Wouldn't it be great if we could all experience that state of equanimity all the time? Well, we can, and we will if we are persistent in our endeavor to wake up from this dream we are having.

The Merriam-Webster dictionary defines forgiveness as, "Excusing for a fault or offense; renouncing anger or resentment against; to absolve from payment." These definitions are fine for our worldly understanding, but they do not describe what true forgiveness is. Each of the dictionary definitions imply that a person is absolving another for some misdeed or fault. This type of forgiveness gives reality to the idea that somebody did something harmful for which they should be forgiven. It puts the cause outside of us and not where it should be, which is within our own mind.

A great practice is seeing the innocence, perfection, and divinity in others and ourselves. This is a very powerful exercise in freeing ourselves from the hell of the ego. It slowly opens up a new way of seeing, which is not related to our physical eyes, but instead this practice strengthens our spiritual vision and supports our understanding of truth.

It is only our false mental concepts and our beliefs that need forgiveness. When you come right down to it, the only thing we ever have to forgive ourselves for is our belief that we are this individual, separate from God. As we practice forgiving ourselves, we naturally begin to forgive the belief that we are separate from God and each other. The absolute truth is that we are totally innocent and have never done anything wrong. We just need to wake up from this dream by taking that first step of dissolving the belief that we are this separated entity through forgiving the illusion. This is the path that will lead us to God and to the realization of who we truly are. **We are the only ones capable of forgiving ourselves. Even a highly developed spiritual being cannot forgive us if we refuse to accept it.** It is said that Jeshua could not perform great miracles for the people in the town where he grew up, because the people could not accept that this person, who grew up in their midst, could be such a great being. When Jeshua healed others, he told them that it was their faith that allowed him to heal them (Matthew 9:22). It was their belief that allowed the energy to flow for the healing to take place. If they were not open to healing, it could not be done. In electricity there is a need to have both a positive and negative polarity in order for energy to flow. To receive a healing, either from another or ourselves, we must be open to the fact that we are deserving of a healing.

Forgiveness will eventually dissolve all belief in this whole physical universe and forgiveness will then become obsolete. In the realm of time, this is still a long, long way away for the great majority of people. In our current sleep state, forgiveness is a great light that will allow us to see more clearly. Our understanding that this world is an illusion and that we have never done anything wrong is the beginning of permanent healing.

The makers of the movie *The Matrix* did a great job in portraying the illusion of the world. We live in a dream world, and yet this dream world is governed by a law of cause and effect. The law of cause and effect does not determine what is good or bad. The universal law of cause and effect operates on the principle that whatever we create mentally, emotionally, and physically is what we must experience. A fully awakened individual invokes the law of cause and effect in a very powerful and positive way. The Dalai Lama, for example, through his belief in non-judgment and forgiveness, invoked the law of cause and effect through forgiveness. This powerful message has affected the world in a very positive way. Unfortunately, in the current situation in the world, the majority of people invoke the law of cause and effect in a way that keeps them caught up in illusion. Wars and everything else in this world are simply a reflection of thoughts and beliefs by individuals, cities, countries, and the entire globe. If we truly forgive ourselves for our belief in good and evil, we would make tremendous strides toward our spiritual freedom. Shakespeare had a deep understanding of truth that was revealed in one of his plays in which Hamlet says, **"There is nothing either good or bad, but thinking makes it so."**

What about a baby who is in a war zone, who has not had a chance to think these horrible thoughts? Why should they be subjected to these cruelties?

We must remember that we have had many dream cycles with many different bodies. This is what metaphysical people refer to as "reincarnations." I prefer to use the term "dream cycles" because it more fully reflects the unreality of our different lifetimes. The dream cycles continue until the spirit awakens. A baby born into a difficult situation is simply experiencing a belief system she carried from previous dream cycles, or the soul may have chosen that experience for a specific life lesson. Just because we leave our bodies at death does not mean we leave all our beliefs, desires, and karma with them. We may not be able to take our money with us when we die, but our karma continues on with us until we have had a chance to neutralize it through our actions and forgiveness. When a child in school fails all his classes in a certain grade, he must return to the same grade after his summer vacation in order to learn the lessons he failed to learn the year before. Life here on Earth is like a school and we keep returning until we have mastered all its lessons. **True mastery comes when a soul is ready to release all identifications with the false individual self.**

Are you saying that no matter what somebody has done, all they have to do is give up their identification with the individual self they believed they were?

Yes, this is an absolute truth, but it is a process of slowly releasing layer after layer of guilt, fears, and false beliefs. You also have to take into consideration that a person who has a lot of karma may not be consciously in a place where they would even consider relinquishing their ego. In a rare case, if they were willing to release all belief in the illusory self, they could transcend the karma they have created. The process of letting go of our identification with the ego is the one true cure for the pain and darkness of this world.

True forgiveness eventually allows a person to realize he has never done anything wrong, that he was simply hypnotized into believing in a world of illusion. Reversing these beliefs will take some time and patience. The important thing is to apply our understanding of the truth in each moment and leave the final release up to God.

What is our part in helping others in the Awakening process?

If you had a child who was having a bad dream and was yelling and kicking the blankets, wouldn't you want to wake the child up and tell her it was just a bad dream? Waking her up does not mean that you are giving credence to the dream. A spiritual person is not helping somebody in the world, she is helping the soul awaken from the dream of the world. Do you see the difference between the two? A person who has awakened from the dream while in a body can be of tremendous assistance in helping others to also awaken.

A person who has spiritual insights, but has still not fully awakened, can also be of great help to others. In helping others to understand the unreal nature of the world, he is helping himself to move closer to the full awakening. Helping others is the same as helping ourselves, because it is our dream and everybody in our dream represents a part of ourselves. We cannot help another without helping ourselves, for we are all One.

What if I don't want to wake up from this dream? Maybe I like it here. Is that wrong?

No, of course not, you have the free will to continue in the cycle of birth and death as long as you desire. There is absolutely no judgment or condemnation of a person if he chooses to remain in the world for as long as he desires. In fact, young souls have to reach a certain stage of ego development before they should even consider a spiritual path. They need the experience of both the dark and the light before they are ready to embark on the spiritual path.

There is no such thing as right or wrong. There is no time limit to the dream of illusion. Each one of us is creating our own individual path in life and each one of us will have to make our own choices as to when we choose to wake up.

Remember, God does not judge, we make all decisions and judgments regarding our individual soul journey. I have mentioned before that even though this world is an illusion, we are still bound by the law of cause and effect or karma. We break free of this law once we fully realize that the identity of the person and body that we believed we were actually never existed, and we no longer identify with that individual. I know it's very hard to accept that the person you think you are in fact is an illusion that never existed. Once we fully realize this Truth, we are in total control of our destiny.

Can you recommend a practice for breaking free of our identification with the person we believe we are?

A great practice is **impersonal self-observation**. This practice will eventually start to free you from not only your false identification but also from this illusionary world. Imagine your true consciousness floating above your body observing everything the false self does, without any identification, judgment, or interpretation. Simply allow the body and mind to do what it is doing while you remain detached to what is going on as the observer of what is happening. When you fully break the identification with the illusory self, you will be free.

Here's a metaphor on the process of forgiveness: One day, a traveler from a distant planet visited another world in which he found all the inhabitants to be insane. The traveler found it very puzzling that the people in this strange world acted in a way that was totally contradictory to their own happiness and peace. He wondered why these people loved pain and suffering so much. He then discovered that the water the people of this world were drinking had been contaminated with a virus that caused insanity. Being a very wise being, the traveler knew exactly what to do to cure their insanity. He went to work and created an anti-virus potion to cure insanity. The potion he concocted was imbued with the vibrations and frequencies needed to counteract the virus. He then put this potion into the drinking water. After drinking the water for some time, the people of this strange world all seemed to come to the same realization. They realized that their insane thoughts, words, and actions, while under the influence of the virus, were bringing about the opposite conditions from what they really wanted to experience. This realization freed them and they departed with the traveler to a world of great love, joy and peace.

True forgiveness is the anti-virus to the insanity of the false ego but remember, we and we alone are the only ones who can make that decision to forgive.

To conclude this important chapter on true forgiveness, I will very briefly explain the paradox of forgiveness. True forgiveness is the ultimate key in freeing ourselves from our own delusion, so it is immensely important that we understand the nature of forgiveness. We are forgiving ourselves and everyone else for something that we or they never did. We are forgiving ourselves and all others for things done in a place that never existed. We are forgiving ourselves and others so that we can be freed from an unreality that never existed. We are forgiving ourselves and others for nothing, in order to remember and inherit everything, which is our birthright. The only thing we ever have to forgive ourselves and others for is the false belief that we are this individual who actually never existed. This is the paradox and the power of true forgiveness. Remember that our true self is eternal and can never die.

We should ponder that last paragraph very deeply because it is of paramount importance that we understand it completely. Understanding and practicing true forgiveness is our key to our spiritual awakening.

Reflection Eleven

One of the hardest things for a person who is very committed to the spiritual journey is to truly forgive himself for a negative action until he realizes the truth, that the person committing the act is not real. The Key to forgiveness is recognizing that sin cannot be substantiated in God's perfect love. Forgiving others who still believe in sin is something an awakened person will do because he knows forgiveness will help that individual let go of the guilt he is feeling. Until a person realizes that the egoic self is not real, he will have a hard time forgiving himself for negative actions. This is especially true for one on the spiritual path striving to awaken. Remember that the law of cause and effect always maintains balance by reflecting back to us what we are creating. Forgiveness is a tool on the spiritual journey but at some point on the journey, the realization will come that the individual person he believed he was, in reality never existed. It is not an easy task to dissolve the ego, but it can be done and must be done if we are to fully awaken spiritually. True change or transformation takes place in our mind.

Twelve

The Inner Child and Innocence

The loss of our true nature of innocence is one of the greatest losses a soul can experience. This loss of innocence took place in the consciousness of the soul when it believed that it had accomplished the separation from God. This is the deepest pain a soul can experience. Unfortunately, most people do not realize that they are extremely wounded because of their forgetfulness that their true nature is to be in Union with God. The awareness of this pain is usually experienced as a soul reaches a high level of spiritual development.

I remember a therapist who was helping me heal my inner child. She told me to go home to try and get in touch with the pain that I experienced as a child because of the loss of my mom. She wanted me to experience this pain because I was not allowed to feel that pain as a child in the orphanage. So when I got home, I went to my meditation room and sat and tried to get in touch with that pain. I was able to experience the pain to a certain degree and a few tears flowed down my cheeks. Then, all of a sudden without even thinking about it, I got in touch with the pain inside me dealing with my separation from God. I had not even tried to contemplate my separation from God, it just happened automatically. The experience was so powerful that tears just poured out of my eyes and I cried like I had never cried before. This went on for about thirty minutes. Even though I had tried to get in touch with my childhood pain, my soul was ready to deal with the deepest pain of all and it happened spontaneously and automatically. The seeming separation from God was our first experience of the loss of the incredible beauty and joy of innocence.

When most people hear the word "innocence," the first association that usually comes to their mind is a very young child. Young children are, for the most part, seen as pure and untainted, in other words: innocent. One passage in the New Testament describes a time when Jeshua was teaching and some children wanted to be near him, but the disciples tried to keep the children away. Jeshua told the disciples not to turn the children away because their very nature reflected those in the Kingdom of Heaven (Matthew 19:14).

What do you think Jeshua meant by that? Does it mean when we finally enter the Kingdom of Heaven we will be as children? In one way, this is true. As we regain the innocent nature we had as a child, we begin to experience the sense of wonderment and timelessness that we had as children. Spiritual maturity and innocence are synonymous. This means that we will regain our innocent nature and be able to experience the joy of innocence. The innocence in children that Jeshua was referring to is a mind that does not know of evil, time, and separation. In this state of innocence, every moment is totally new and boredom is impossible. Unfortunately, in our day and age, children are exposed to so much negative information so early in their lives that it doesn't take long for them to lose their childhood innocence.

I remember when I was a child how everything was so new and exciting to me. The colors were so much more vibrant and alive. Everything was happening in the present moment and I wasn't concerned with the past or the future. I didn't have the greatest of childhoods, but during that innocent period, everything was a mystery which opened up a whole new world of possibilities. I remember playing with the wind and chasing butterflies with total abandonment, freedom, and joy.

Most of us remember the period of time when we believed in Santa Claus. Wasn't it a joy as a child to believe in someone so magical with his flying reindeer? As a child in the orphanage I would run out to the yard on Christmas Day to see if I could find the reindeer prints in the snow. Even in the orphanage, the spirit of Christmas was alive as we waited in great anticipation for Christmas Eve and Christmas Day. In the orphanage, we were usually only given one present for Christmas but what we were given was cherished. One year I got a toy car that would wind up as I pushed the wheels against the floor and then I would let it go and it moved across the floor with lights flashing. It was a real treasure to me. As I write about it, I get a very clear picture of that time and feeling. If physical childhood innocence can bring such joy from something so insignificant, just imagine what we have in store for us as perfectly innocent spirits in God's infinite Kingdom.

I also remember when I started to lose my innocence and entered into the world of time and fear. In the orphanage, the nun who was in charge of us kids was a very sadistic person. If we did anything that she considered wrong, no matter how innocent it was, she would take us aside and beat us with a piece of wood about 1 inch thick x 3 inches wide. We would have to pull our pants down and lay over a bed while she would hit us with all her might on our butt. It was very painful and we were not allowed to make a sound while we were being beaten. We would receive anywhere from ten to fifty whacks, depending on the mood of the nun. Anyway, this nun would often make me wait the whole day before beating me, which meant that during that day I dreaded the arrival of evening when I would receive the beating. It was at this point when I became familiar with the concept of time as I anxiously waited for the boom to be lowered. I clearly remember the anxiety I felt during those days. I dreaded the waiting almost more than the beating, but the worst part was losing that childlike innocence. You might want to reflect back to a time when you began to lose your innocence.

Later in life as I entered my spiritual journey I realized why I had chosen to experience such a traumatic childhood. I realized the nun was only playing out a part in my dream, as I was playing out a part in her dream. It would be foolish of me to blame her for the trauma I went through because if it had not been her, it would have been somebody else. I chose to go through that experience for a certain reason. To judge the nun as being at fault would entangle me in that karma, rather than freeing me. Forgiveness of our self and others is the only path of liberation from any painful experience.

We are probably all familiar with the story of Adam and Eve in the Garden of Eden. In this story, Adam and Eve were told that they could eat from any tree in the garden except for one tree in the very center. They were told that if they ate from the tree of the knowledge of good and evil, they would surely die. A serpent then came along and tempted Eve, telling her that she would not die if she ate from the tree, but that she would become as God. The fruit of the tree in the center of the garden was very tempting, so Eve ate the fruit and gave some to Adam to eat. The story goes on to say that when they ate the apple, their eyes were opened and they saw that they were naked and so they hid themselves. The story states that God then cast Adam and Eve out of the garden because of their disobedience (Genesis 3).

The story of Adam and Eve is taken very literally by many religious groups, but its symbolism reveals a much deeper understanding of what happened. I will not go into detail of what all the symbols mean but I want to give you an overall picture of the true meaning of the story of Adam and Eve and how this relates to the loss of our innocence. Adam and Eve represent the souls who, through the gift of free will, decided to journey into the darkness of creation. This decision caused a deep sleep to fall upon them. In the darkness, the souls seemed to fragment into many parts or individuals. Many souls are dreaming similar experiences as ours in different worlds and different realities. Our focus for now is on this world, which is the densest plane of illusion for a soul to enter.

Adam and Eve were very innocent while they were in the Garden of Eden. The Garden represents our conscious Unity with God and the unlimited love, joy and innocence, which are our natural states. While in this state of innocence, there was no concept of good and evil. The concept of separation and time were also nonexistent in this state. Remember, we were created in the image of God. In fact, we were made from God's own Consciousness. We each had our own unique awareness of what was taking place.

The souls were created in perfect balance, with each soul containing both positive and negative polarities. The positive polarity is considered a male energy, whereas the negative polarity is considered female. The positive polarity was more outgoing and mental, whereas the negative polarity was more receptive and feeling. The serpent tempted the negative polarity of the soul, telling her that she would be as God if she ate from the tree of the knowledge of good and evil. The serpent represents the first appearance of the false ego that lured us into illusion. The ego caused certain souls to question the nature of God as the Creator. This intruder in Heaven convinced the soul that it could create a place outside of God, where it could be the creator and take the place of God. In this dark, illusory state, the ego was free to be in charge. Now remember that the false ego is not a real thing but is rather an illusionary concept that came into being as a result of our desire to experience life separate from God. The ego succeeded in tempting the soul to create an unreal state in which the ego could now live out its lie. The ego's existence is totally dependent on us experiencing and believing that the separation from God is real. All evil and darkness are the result of the illusionary ego.

How is it possible that something like the ego could come into existence in the perfect Mind of God?

It is not really possible and that is why I keep saying that this world is all a dream, it is not real. This world is no more real than a fleeting thought that arises and disappears in your mind. As I said before, don't spend too much time thinking about it because it can be very confusing. The time will come when our conscious expansion has reached a point where enough of our inner light is illuminating our mind which will allow us to see through the illusion and be free.

Ever since our self-eviction from the Garden of Eden, we have been trying to regain our positive/negative balance so that we might return. We seek each other for relationships, hoping that the relationship will bring the balance and joy that we lost a long time ago. The true balance is within each soul, as each one of us in our true nature is a perfect balance of female and male polarities. The Mystical Marriage between the two polarities will take place when divine wisdom and perfect love unite in the soul. *A Course in Miracles* refers to spiritual union as a Holy Relationship.

On the contrary, a relationship based on need and desire is referred to as a "special relationship." In the special relationship, each partner is trying to get something from the other to make himself or herself feel whole. This will never happen in such a relationship because special relationships are based on a need that can only be filled from within each individual.

In the Holy Relationship, there is an understanding by the two souls that spiritual awakening and expansion is their goal. In the Holy Relationship, there is an effort by both parties to see the other as being perfectly innocent and divine. Through acknowledging the divinity of their partner, both of them are awakened. So, in the Holy Relationship, the other is our savior as we are theirs.

We can have this Holy Relationship with everyone we meet. We can practice superimposing over their physical appearance the spiritual reality of who they really are. As we do this our vision adapts to see ourselves in the same light.

There is a huge gap between Heaven and Earth, but there have been many great souls who have created bridges between the two. Every soul who spiritually awakens makes it that much easier for those who are to follow. I especially honor the life of Jeshua Ben Joseph because at the time he was born the karma and darkness on Earth was so strong that Earth was heading into a place of darkness from which it might not have been able to return. Through his willingness to go through the crucifixion, he was able to create a bridge from illusion to reality, from hate to love. This bridge is available to all. I can hear some thinking, "Here's another Christian who thinks the only way is through Jesus Christ." I am not saying that a person must believe in or follow the teachings of Jeshua in order to return home. There have been many other great saints who have also sacrificed their lives and created bridges between Heaven and Earth. Any true spiritual teacher can lead others across the bridge. Jeshua and the other great saints don't care if you acknowledge what they did, they only care that you return. It can be through the path of Buddhism, Judaism, Hinduism or any other path that will lead you home. I can tell you that I understand what Jeshua accomplished through his life here on Earth and I am eternally grateful for the path he has opened up to us.

The story of Adam and Eve states that once they ate the apple, their eyes were opened (Genesis 3:7). It would be more accurate to say that after eating the apple, their eyes were closed. The eyes that were opened were the illusory physical eyes that perceive life through the vision of duality and separation. This distorted vision was the beginning of struggle and pain.

Our technology has evolved to the point that a person with poor eyesight can have their vision corrected with a laser procedure. The truth is that regardless of how great a person sees physically, he is still blind if he has not had his spiritual vision opened. We've probably all been in a car where the windows have been iced over on a cold night. Without defrosting the windows, it is impossible to see clearly out the glass. Our vision is so obstructed by the ice that it would be very dangerous to drive without the windows being defrosted. The spiritually asleep individual is like somebody driving with their windows all iced over. He will bump into so many things and even have a bad accident. If we use only our physical vision, then we will continue to walk through life blindly. We will not really know what to do or which direction to take. Our spiritual sight allows us to see through the illusion of the physical world.

It is a strange world and state of consciousness that we have created for ourselves, in which we have an easier time accepting the idea that we are guilty, rather than accepting the truth of our innocence. Observe yourself without any concepts or judgments about what is happening in your life. Simply observe that character that you have identified with all your life as if you were observing a figment of your imagination, which is all it is. Constantly seek to remember that in reality you are and always have been in total Union with God. Do this and you will be well on your way to spiritual liberation. Contemplate the truth, repeat affirmations based on spiritual truths, practice seeing the truth wherever you are and the darkness will slowly dissipate, revealing a most beautiful sunrise.

Most of us have watched a moth flying around a flame. The moth is very attracted to the flame but if it gets too close it is immediately consumed by it. Our spiritual desire is what attracts us to the divine flame of love but our ego tries to frighten us by telling us that we will die if we get too close. In a sense, the ego is correct in that everything false within us will die and we will be fully awakened into the state of perfect and total Union with God. For the great majority of the people on Earth at this time, a gradual unfoldment has been taking place over many lifetimes, which is leading to a great awakening. When this happens, the false ego and illusion will completely disappear into the nothingness from whence it came.

It is very difficult not to love an innocent child, unless the darkness in a person is so thick that very little light is shining in their mind. You've heard the saying that charity begins at home. Begin by loving yourself and accepting the pure innocence of your being. You are deserving of everything, without any limits. Everything you deserve is permeated with pure and perfect Love. **You deserve everything because you are and always have been perfectly innocent in your Oneness with God.** Find your innocence by seeing it in others.

Throughout this book I have been speaking of the need to completely transform our way of thinking but don't make the mistake of being too hard on yourself. One of my greatest lessons was learning how to let go and relax and not feel I had to attain perfection. I had an ascetic attitude for a good portion of my spiritual journey. We should be easy on ourselves, love ourselves, and allow others to love us. We have nothing of which we should feel guilty or ashamed. **It is out of our false belief in the ego that we create guilt and shame. We simply need to understand the truth about our innocence. Discipline may be beneficial for a short time in order to gain a spiritual foundation but at a certain point of our spiritual journey we need to focus on the fact that we are and always have been innocent and thus honor and fully accept ourselves in this Holy Light.**

Understanding who we are and living in accordance with this truth is the path to our awakening. Even before we complete this journey, we will begin to feel the joy, peace, love and light that will fill our whole being. This will make it so much easier to let go more fully. Be a happy face. Renounce all ideas that God desires sacrifice, because that is the opposite of truth. Observe happy young children at play and that will give us some idea as to the attitude we should seek to emulate. As we accept the fact that we are perfectly innocent, we will make room for true joy to fill our whole being.

Reflection Twelve

Our conscious Unity with God is unlimited love, joy and innocence, which are our natural states. The seeming separation from God was our first experience of the loss of the incredible beauty and joy of innocence. True innocence is such a beautiful state in which worries and sadness are not possible. Innocence is a state of mind that will come to a soul who has finally realized the truth. We are totally innocent; we have never done anything wrong.

We appear to be existing in a holographic projection of the mind created by a desire of the soul to experience consciousness outside the Mind of God. Of course, this is impossible since God is all there is.

All souls who seek to awaken from this dark dream and return to the innocence of our true nature must relinquish the identification with the false self. The full release of this false belief is happening more and more in this third dimensional experience. The simple acceptance of this truth has opened the way for souls to release the illusion of the false self. The final joyous result of this will be a state of pure Innocence and Love.

Thirteen

Letting Go

One of the first teachings I received in the Holy Order of MANS was to **"Let go and let God."** This is a very simple phrase, but there is an infinite depth to it when the meaning is fully realized.

Many of us are so used to trying to control our lives that it takes a great deal of faith to fully turn over the very essence of our lives to God. It is in times of trials and dealing with obstacles that we find out if we are really willing to release the steering wheel to God. During Jeshua's ministry, people would come up to him with problems about different facets of their lives. Jeshua told them to look at birds of the air and the flowers in the field and how there was no effort on their part and yet they unfolded in all their beauty and splendor. He told the people that if the flowers of the field—which are only a temporary manifestation of beauty—are taken care of, then how much more will God take care of them, who are eternal children of God? (Matthew 6:25-34.)

Having the trust to let go and accept that our needs will be taken care of requires that we have a connection to our heart. It is in being connected with our heart that we begin to allow the powerful flow of creation to manifest in our lives. It cannot be done with the mind alone. The mind is normally dealing with our exterior life, whereas the heart is dealing with our inner reality and our connection to the Divine. Our connection with our heart opens the way for creation to flow through us and empowers us so that we can fulfill the purpose for which we entered the realm of Earth. There is a perfect flow in creation that we can connect with by attuning ourselves with our heart. This flow of creation is sort of like a powerful river of Light, Life and Love, which will automatically take us to God if we are willing to let go and let God guide us. The *Heart* is the conduit through which this pure energy enters the physical realm. There is no limit to this powerful flow and there is no limit to a soul who has fully connected with his Sacred Heart. This is why it is so important to get in touch with our heart. The heart is our connection between the spirit and the physical.

The heart is a most amazing organ and it is the most sacred and holy place through which we can contact and connect with God. Even though it seems that it is our brain through which we respond to life, it is the heart that is the true director of our journey through life if we allow it to be. Through quantum physics and our advanced technology, it has been discovered that the heart is the true brain of the body. The world has been led to believe that it is the brain that directs all functions in the body but that is not true. The heart directs the brain and the brain then transmits those directions to the body. The field of energy that the heart produces is many times more powerful than what the brain creates and thus exerts a greater influence on all our bodies. Once a person reaches a certain level of spiritual development, he will begin to be guided by the Heart. The Heart is the sanctuary where God dwells. In meditation we can make contact with the Creator through our Heart. When you enter meditation, focus on your heart. Allow the heart to guide you in all areas of your life.

Years ago in meditation, I was automatically guided to focus on the heart and breathe very rapidly into this most sacred place. My breath was very strong and without effort. The feelings that were coming from my heart during this time were very beautiful. This automatic breath into my heart went on for many months. I was not sure exactly what was happening but I sensed that the heart was being attuned and energized by the powerful rapid breathwork that was taking place almost automatically. At this time in my spiritual process, my meditations were spontaneously guided and always completely focused on my heart.

Letting go and letting God is an act of great faith. Many times a person has to reach the bottom before they realize that there has to be a better way. It is at this point that many turn to God and ask for help, not knowing how help is going to manifest. They have come to a point of surrendering. The last thing the ego wants to do is relinquish control and thus the stage is set for the spiritual aspirant's inner battle with the ego. This is the most difficult part of our spiritual journey. It is stage three of our journey, which I spoke about in an earlier chapter.

As I have noted earlier in the book, a large portion of my spiritual journey in this lifetime was very difficult and painful. The last few years of my journey were interspersed with times of deep peace and times of intense changes going on within me. I had no idea where life was taking me, I simply let go of all expectations. I had opened the doorway to my heart and had surrendered completely. I actually experienced faster growth during my most difficult challenges by accepting these challenges as steppingstones toward my spiritual awakening. Inwardly I knew that everything was happening in perfect synchronicity and in perfect harmony with the Will of God. I didn't have to do anything, except simply be and do whatever was placed in front of me. I was fully aware that even the difficulties I encountered were a gift which allowed me to let go of even deeper layers of pain and false beliefs.

There comes a time in a person's spiritual development where she realizes that there is nothing she needs to do in order to awaken. More than that, she recognizes that as long as she feels she has to do something to awaken, she will keep the awakening at a distance. As long as a soul considers themselves to be a seeker they will not find the truth. At a certain point we must accept the truth of who we are and not keep seeking something that is right in front of us. As long as we believe that this world and all its pain is something real that needs to be escaped, then we are accepting the illusion as truth.

You keep saying we need to act and think in a certain way in order to free ourselves from this illusion and now you are telling us that we don't have to do anything. Exactly what is it that we are to do?

I mentioned that a person has to be at a certain stage in their spiritual development for this idea of not doing anything to be appropriate. If a person has not reached this stage of spiritual development, then this idea would not be appropriate, nor would it be helpful to the individual.

In the beginning and middle stages of the spiritual journey a lot of spiritual, mental, emotional, and physical preparation is absolutely necessary but there will come a time when the spiritual seeker must let go of seeking and accept the truth. As long as we are seeking something, we have not yet found it. A state of knowing must be reached before the seeking ends. At this point a person does not have to do anything except to be in the present moment. Whatever the present moment brings is accepted fully without any resistance, knowing that whatever is taking place in that moment is exactly what is needed for her greater awakening. She has reached a level of faith in which she knows that she is taken care of completely. She knows that even though she has not fully awakened spiritually, that all things needed for her awakening have been accomplished and is simply waiting for God to take the final step that brings about the full Union with God.

Something that is extremely important to understand for anyone on the spiritual path is that their first and foremost duty is to heal themselves. Once we are healed, we automatically radiate the spiritual light that can help to awaken others. Honoring ourselves is extremely important. Shakespeare, in one of his sonnets, touched on this idea when he wrote, "This above all: to thine own self be true."

As we walk on this journey, we will be used in a way that is perfectly suited for us. God has a plan for each of us in this process of awakening. It is as if all lightworkers are each a piece of a giant puzzle. We all have our particular place and purpose in this puzzle. The puzzle cannot be fully completed until each one of us has fulfilled our part. Jeshua said that a candle is not lit to be put under the bed or under a bushel but rather it is placed where it can give light to the entire house (Matthew 5:14-16). An awakened person will be guided to be exactly where he is supposed to be. He will be placed in a situation that will allow the light within him to influence the souls he was intended to contact. The awakened ones are kind and compassionate. Some may appear to be very unconventional. The one thing that is different about these souls is that they know that **none of this is real and so there is nothing to struggle against.** It is their awareness of the truth that sets them apart, even though most people would not be able to tell them apart from the masses.

An exercise to help us remember who we are is as follows: Close your eyes, focus on your breathing and allow the mind to cease all thinking. It may take a little while but wait until your mind is completely still. Now with the mind very still with no thoughts, notice that you are still aware. This awareness, void of all thoughts and identifications, is a state that can help lead you to the realization of who you truly are.

In the beginning of our spiritual journey, it takes a tremendous effort of will to swim against the current of the mass mind of this world. The belief system of the world forms a strong current in which many younger souls are swept along. We will not lose anything that is real, only that which is an illusion. **That which is real can never be lost.**

How would one go about swimming against the current of mass consciousness?

A person must first want the truth above all else before he can begin the process of waking up from this dream. Understanding Truth reveals that the beliefs and thinking of the mass mind of the world are perpetuating an illusionary existence. Truth will reveal to us who we really are and what we are not. This realization automatically puts us on a different path, which is the opposite direction of the mass mind of this world.

Many believe that the crucifixion of Jeshua has saved them and all they have to do is believe this and they are free. Jeshua did open a door into Heaven for all but it was mainly through his resurrection that this door was opened. He brought into this world a great light that made it easier to follow a path out of this illusion. **Each one of us has to make the decision and effort to seek and become the light ourselves.** As I said before, it doesn't mean we have to become an ascetic, it means putting the truth first. The truth is not that complicated. The question is: how much do we want it?

When I joined the Order, I met my first teacher, Father Paul, who told us about a student who came to him one day and complained that he felt like he didn't know anything. Father Paul replied, "Ah, so you finally got it." He was informing the student that by letting go of everything he thought he knew, he was making room for the truth to enter. Father Paul continually taught that we must become as nothing in order to clear the way for Spiritual Enlightenment.

Our spiritual journey in this world is a process in which we battle an illusionary foe. After many battles, we finally realize that the foe we were fighting against was our own false belief system. At this stage we understand the words of Jeshua when he said, "Resist not evil" (Matthew 5:39). By no longer resisting, we completely give up our self-efforts and allow God to bring us to the final step of full spiritual awakening. This is a long process of self-effort and finally letting go so that God can complete the process. Let your heart be your guide and you can never go wrong. At some point we will find it very amusing that we have been fighting against something that does not exist in order to gain everything that exists eternally.

Becoming nothing in the world has nothing to do with our material assets or position. As I have shared many times, the transformation and the resurrection all take place in our mind, or more accurately, in our heart. It is in the mind where all the work is done but it is in our heart where we experience our Union with God.

In truth, separation from God is an absolute impossibility since God is all that is. Where could we possibly go to separate ourselves from God? We need to be very vigilant anytime the slightest disturbance arises in our minds or bodies and not identify with it but simply observe it without any identification with it. Whenever I experienced any kind of emotional upset, I would take time and observe the emotion without any judgment. I found that by giving it attention without any judgment or interpretation, the effect of the emotion would lessen.

The spiritually awakened individuals who have taken on the mission of working within the illusion have great compassion. They know of the hardships and suffering going on in the world but in order to help others out of this nightmare, they must stand on the rock of Truth. They cannot lend validity to the illusion by seeing it as true and blaming and judging others for what is happening. It also doesn't mean they condone what is happening. They recognize the dream for what it is and at the same time provide any help they can to others according to how they are guided. **A spiritually awakened being has compassion for both the victim and the perpetrator without any judgment.** When the Enlightened state is realized, there is no judgment because of the knowing that this is just a dream and that we all have been on both sides of the drama. **An enlightened mind has transcended both the darkness and the light with the knowing that they are two sides of a whole. You cannot have one without the other.**

This next truth might be difficult for some to accept but we and we alone have created the whole world we seem to be participating in. We and we alone are responsible for forgiving this whole world that we have created. As long as we project guilt on anyone or anything, we are in a sense projecting that guilt unto ourselves through our judgment. Only after we have forgiven ourselves completely for the judgments we have projected onto the world will we be able to reach a more expanded state of consciousness.

Quantum physicists have discovered that any thought that was ever imagined resulted in an effect where that imagination could find expression. The quantum world, with all its many dimensions, parallel universes and infinite possibilities is all very fascinating but as Jeshua said, "Keep thine eye single and thy whole body shall be filled with Light" (Matthew 6:22-23). All knowledge that we need to further our spiritual advancement will be available to us each moment as we sincerely walk the spiritual path. Every one of us is responsible for the entire physical universe. It's all our dream that we seem to inhabit. We are all experiencing a totally different universe because of our different states of mind and what we believe. Our beliefs determine what is projected on the screen of our mind. Just notice how people react differently to headlines in the news. A person caught up in illusion will react very differently to a situation than one who is awake. An awakened person will not react but will respond to a situation in the way in which he is led. Each of us has our unique perspective and experience of the world because of the fragmentation of the mind. This fragmentation took place at the seeming time of the separation. Therefore, when an individual fully awakens spiritually, the fragmentation of the mind dissolves and he sees through the eyes of Oneness.

We shouldn't be concerned with time but instead put our efforts into focusing on *letting go* in the present moment. The statement that "there is nothing new under the sun" is correct (Ecclesiastes 1:9). The past, present and the future have already come and gone. It all happened in less than the blink of an eye.

Most people have heard of the idea of living in the Now. Here is a spiritual gem that can really help you in *letting go* of the illusion: **The most important thing you will ever do is what you are doing at this very moment.** If you can perceive the value of this statement you will have a very powerful practice, which will dramatically speed up your spiritual progress.

If there is nothing we can do outside of Now, wouldn't you say that Now is all we have? If Now is all we have, shouldn't we give everything we have to this very special eternal moment? The future and the past are just that, so the only time we have is this current moment. Time is one of the biggest illusions of all. We can speed up the process of awakening by *letting go* and practicing being in the present moment. I mentioned before that the ego cannot exist outside the illusionary realm of time. The ego needs our belief and involvement in time to exist. Living in the Now is a very powerful spiritual practice to dissolve the ego.

The current moment contains everything we could possibly desire for our fulfillment, because God dwells in the timeless state of Now. Letting go of time and being in the present moment is an extremely important spiritual practice.

The problem that the vast majority of people have is that a great deal of their physical, emotional, and mental energy is tied up in the past or the future. Very little of their energy is left to use in the only time there is, which is Now.

We should all do our part in trying to make this world a more peaceful and loving place to live by spreading good will to everybody we meet. A person who has awakened from the realm of time is spreading the Light of Truth just by his very presence. In his activities, the light in him will continue to shine forth and be a healing presence to the mind of the world.

Jeshua and many other great spiritual beings came into the world of form to bring the Light of Truth into the minds and hearts of their brothers and sisters so that they would awaken from the world. It wasn't so much to change the illusion but to awaken others from the illusion. Jeshua said, "Render unto Caesar what is Caesar's and unto God what is God's" (Matthew 22:21). These great beings came to awaken those who were ready to move on in their spiritual evolution. The mistake the church and other religious institutions have made is that they have made these spiritual beings special and different from the average person. That is not at all what these great beings came to teach. They came to show us that we too are the Way, the Truth, and the Light. They came to shatter the false beliefs and illusion of this world. The light they brought is like a great seed that was planted in the earth. This seed has now grown into a great tree of light which is now encompassing and giving light to the whole world. The light they brought into the world has made it so much easier for humanity to understand the truth. Jeshua said he was in the world but not of it (John 17:14).

The great spiritual beings knew this world was not real, but because we believed in this illusion, they came to plant the seed of light so that we might wake up from this dream.

Let me give you another analogy to help make this idea a little clearer. Imagine that several billion people were trapped in a very dark, immensely large building with no light and had no idea how to get out. They were afraid to take a step, not knowing if some abyss lay before them. A group of 10,000 political leaders was in charge of coming up with a plan to help the people out of the dark building but since they were living in the same darkness as the others, they were trying to operate from a weakened state of mind and were limited in helping everyone. They came up with many plans and theories, but nothing seemed to change the fact that people were trapped in the dark. Now imagine that unbeknownst to these people, each one of them had an unlit candle on their person. Some even talked about the mysterious candle but did nothing to light it, nor did they teach others to light it because it had become a mental theory. So the 10,000 leaders discussed how everyone might get out, but since nobody knew the way out, their theories became meaningless.

In the far corners of the building, a few people discovered their candles and learned how to light them. The light from these candles allowed people around them to see clearly enough to start moving toward the exit of the building. Who provided the greater assistance to the people trapped in the building: the 10,000 who had all kinds of theories on how to get out, or the few who actually provided light for others to see?

Trying to change things in the outer world without changing the inner, is like a person whose house is on fire and tries to fix it by rearranging all the furniture in the house. Of course, this does nothing to address the cause. The fire keeps burning and destroying the house as the furniture is being moved around.

We've all probably seen professional magicians perform acts that seemed impossible, only to find out later that the trick was done with mirrors or some other gimmick. This is exactly what the ego has done to make this world seem real. It has done such a great job that the whole world has swallowed the ego's lie hook, line, and sinker. One tool that all magicians use is distraction. They distract the audience by doing something with the right hand, while the left hand can manipulate something in order to make it appear magical. The ego has set up everything in this world as a way of distracting us from the truth. These distractions can be anything from money, fame, disease, and death. The ego will create any circumstance in order to keep us believing that this world is real. Even though the ego seems to be a good magician, we must remember that it was *us* who seemingly gave life to the ego and our own inner light will free us from that illusion.

The advancement of our technology allows us to experience virtual tours that seem so real. Our technology is becoming so advanced that when a person experiences the virtual effects, it is as if the person is actually having the experience. If you contemplate the idea of how real some of these virtual experiences seem to be, it might help you to gain some insight into the illusion of this world.

Many have to reach a spiritual crisis before they are ready to let go and let God. We need to reach a state of mind in which we realize that **this world is a total illusion, it does not exist!** When a person finally comes to the realization that he really does not know anything, including who he is or what this world is all about, he will have reached a state of readiness to fully receive the truth. We, our ego, must become nothing to attain everything. God has given us everything and the ego has given us the illusion of pain and separation. Which one are we going to choose?

How can we function in this world if we let go of all we believe?

You will function in a much more efficient way than you ever thought possible and it can eventually become effortless. As we get our unbalanced egos out of the way and let go, we allow the Power, Intelligence and Love of God to flow through us, producing maximum efficiency in all we do. Letting go of illusion brings us into a state of Awakening into that which we Are. This is the Key to the Kingdom of Heaven.

Reflection Thirteen

Letting go of the illusionary self who we believe we are is the very simple yet powerful process to the remembrance of our true self. You can escalate the process of letting go by observing, without any judgment or interpretation, what is taking place in the moment. Through this impersonal self-observation, you are slowly dissolving that which is keeping you from the joy and love within your own self. Letting go of the ego takes total dedication and effort to accomplish.

We must become nothing to attain everything.

Having the trust to let go and accept that our needs will be taken care of requires that we have a connection to our heart. You will receive plenty of help and support from the spiritual realm. The mind is normally dealing with our exterior life, whereas the heart is dealing with our inner reality and our connection to the Divine.

This flow of creation is sort of like a powerful river of Light, Life, and Love, which will automatically take us to God if we are willing to let go and let God guide us. Be patient with yourself in this process and the benefits will be without measure.

The Summit

**EVERYTHING THAT EVER EXISTED
OR EVER WILL EXIST IS GOD.
THERE IS NOTHING THAT EXISTS THAT IS NOT GOD.**

What is truth? This is a question that Pontius Pilate asked Jeshua before the crucifixion. He knew of Jeshua's teachings and asked him, "What is truth?" Jeshua remained silent as he knew that Pilate would not be able to understand (John 18:38). Truth is always ready and waiting for a soul when he is ready to awaken. There are so many versions of truth in the different religious and philosophical arenas of the world.

So, *what is truth*? Truth could be summed up in two words: **GOD IS.**

These two words are the very essence of what truth is. Everything that ever existed or ever will exist is God. There is nothing that exists that is not God.

The truth really is that simple when our minds are ready and clear and we have released the belief that we are separate and guilty for some imagined sin.

The dream of separation from God happened over millions of years and we are in this long process before the last soul experiences the full awakening.

We have already been through countless worlds and dimensions, through thousands and thousands of incarnations.

In this illusionary realm of time, we have free will and thus it is up to each soul as to how long she will take to let go of her identification with the illusory ego and awaken to reality.

We are now in an unprecedented time in which everything has been prepared for souls to awaken en masse. There are so many spiritual graces available at this current time on Earth.

Pray for the strength and wisdom that will lead you to spiritual light and absolute freedom.

I have created many analogies and stories in this book to bring Light to those of different levels of spiritual awareness.

I wrote about an experience I had at the beginning of my spiritual journey in this life, in which I was told to remain simple and I would reach my destination. The spiritual truth is very simple, but it is our identification with the ego that makes everything so complicated.

I would like to reflect on some truths that I have contemplated which can serve as a light throughout your spiritual journey:

1. We are One with God, perfectly pure and innocent and nothing can alter that truth, regardless of the distorted perceptions of how bad we think we are.

2. The truth is: we have never done anything wrong, we have simply fallen asleep spiritually.

3. As your spiritual light becomes brighter you will see things through a different lens and realize there is nothing to feel guilty about.

4. It is through our sincere intention and will to dissolve the illusory self that we will be given the grace through which we can awaken from this dream.

5. What we believe determines what we experience in life.

6. One of the most important practices is that of forgiveness. In truth, we are forgiving ourselves for something that is not real and actually never happened. We forgive ourselves for temporarily falling asleep and believing the dream we are having is real.

7. To reach the state of Full Enlightenment, which is the object of the spiritual journey, we must become the observer, letting go of all judgment and accepting all that is happening with non-resistance.

8. Awakening and following the path of Truth brings its own challenges because we are swimming against the current of the false beliefs of the mass mind of humanity.

We are all unique and are all having very different life experiences. During different stages of our journey, one person's truth may not be true for another. It is the thoughts and beliefs of a soul that determine what truth is for them.

I truly honor and am grateful to all the lightworkers on the planet today and to those who have come before us such as Buddha, Jeshua, and many more. The journey through the darkness of this world is not an easy path to walk and lightworkers are celebrated by the ascended souls and the angelic realms above. This path can be very difficult and sometimes it may seem like we are not getting anywhere but keep the faith, for we are in a time when the doors to the higher realms are open wide for all of us. We are truly in an age in which we can take that final step of transcending duality and remembering the great truth of who we truly are.

Enlightenment means to radiate and be One with the Light, which changes our consciousness and perception of how we see ourselves, others, and the world.

When a soul reaches a certain level of spiritual development, all judgments and attachments to the world of illusion will begin to dissolve. She will understand she is in the world, but not of it.

In my current state of consciousness, I operate with an awareness that I am in this world but not of it. I experience an empty mind, deep inner stillness and I have dismantled the illusion of separation and judgment. I live in the flow of Union with God. I constantly sing, hum, laugh and I have returned to my innocence. I do not (only) rely on reason to direct my life, I completely accept that God is living through me and guiding my life in all things.

Many blessings will fill our life on our journey back home into our Oneness with God. In the final stages of this journey, we will fully realize we never left our Oneness with God.

I pray that as you travel this Sacred Path, that Grace will fill your life in every facet of your Journey.

My Love to All of You on your return back home.

Recommended Resources and Further Reading

Hawkins, David R. *Power Versus Force: An Anatomy of Consciousness: the Hidden Determinants of Human Behavior.* Carlsbad, CA: Hay House Inc., 2014.

Howard, Vernon. *The Mystic Path to Cosmic Power.* Parker Publishing Company, 1979.

Kribbe, Pamela (Channeled). *The Jeshua Channelings: Christ Consciousness in a New Era.* Booklocker.com, Inc., 2008.

Perron, Mari (First Receiver). *A Course of Love: Combined Volume: The Course, The Treatises, The Dialogues (Including Dialogue Unveiled).* The Center for A Course of Love. Take Heart Publications, North San Juan, California, 2014, 2019. *A Course of Love* (Book One) was first published by New World Library, Novato, California. *A Course of Love* (Book One), *A Course of Love: The Treatises* (Book Two), and *A Course of Love: The Dialogues* (Book Three) were subsequently published as separate volumes by Course of Love Publications, St. Paul, Minnesota.

Renard, Gary. *The Disappearance of the Universe: Straight Talk about Illusions, Past Lives, Religion, Sex, Politics, and the Miracles of Forgiveness* (Revised edition). Hay House, Inc., 2004. First published in 2002 and 2003.

Schucman, Helen (Scribe). *A Course in Miracles: Combined Volume* (Third

Edition). Mill Valley, CA: the Foundation for Inner Peace. The Foundation for *A Course in Miracles*, www.facim.org, 2007. *A Course in Miracles* was first published in three volumes in June 1976 by the Foundation for Inner Peace.

Shanti Christo Foundation. *The Way of Mastery: The Way of the Heart, The Way of Transformation, The Way of Knowing* (Enhanced Edition). Sacramento, CA: Shanti Christo Foundation, www.shantichristo.com, 2005, 2020. Jayem (Jon Marc Hammer) was the "very reluctant channel" of the Way of Mastery, which unfolded over years through an extraordinary encounter with Jeshua (Jesus) in 1987 (Retrieved from https://artoflivingretreatcenter.org/faculty-members/jayem-jon-marc-hammer/). This material is not quoted or paraphrased in this book, yet it is recommended for further reading.

The Holy Order of MANS: https://holyorderofmans.org. "Dedicated to teaching and living The Ancient Mystery Teachings in today's world."

Tolle, Eckhart. *The Power of Now*. Novato, CA: New World Library, 1999. Originally published in Vancouver, B.C., Canada by Namaste Publishing Inc., 1997. Preface to the paperback edition, copyright by Eckhart Tolle, 2004.

Gil Esquibel

Gil Esquibel's journey began in 1969 when he had an experience in which Jeshua, the man known as Jesus, appeared to him in the hills of Northern California. Shortly after that experience he was guided to join a Spiritual Order in San Francisco, which is where the process of "dying to his personal ego" began.

In 1971 as an ordained priest he began to have many deep spiritual experiences and realizations of who we truly are. Gil has been singly focused on experiencing his Union with God for over fifty years resulting in a powerful transformative manifestation of Self Realization.

His purpose is to manifest this truth, opening a path for humanity out of the darkness of illusion into the Light.

"I have experienced the amazing realization that I am God and that all people and everything that has ever existed is God.

I was guided to write this book to get the truth of who we truly are to all those who are seeking and ready for the truth which will set them free."

—Gil Esquibel

Gil Esquibel and Ashleigh F. Torres share a love and adoration for God. Their purpose is to embody Unconditional Love and the ability to balance a formless life in what we perceive as form and limited.

www.ingramcontent.com/pod-product-compliance
Lightning Source LLC
Chambersburg PA
CBHW020246130626
46549CB00005B/2092